Quick and Easy Crafts

Wire Jewellery

18 step-by-step projects – simple to make, stunning results

DOROTHY WOOD

NEW
HOLLAND

This edition published in 2006

First published in 2005 by
New Holland Publishers (UK) Ltd
London • Cape Town • Sydney • Auckland
www.newhollandpublishers.com

Garfield House, 86–88 Edgware Road, London W2 2EA, United Kingdom

80 McKenzie Street, Cape Town 8001, South Africa

Level 1, Unit 4, 14 Aquatic Drive, Frenchs Forest, NSW 2086, Australia

218 Lake Road, Northcote, Auckland, New Zealand

ISBN-10: 1 84537 667 6
ISBN-13: 978 1 84537 667 3

Senior Editors: Clare Sayer, Steffanie Brown
Production: Hazel Kirkman
Design: Glyn Bridgewater
Photographer: Shona Wood
Editorial Direction: Rosemary Wilkinson

10 9 8 7 6 5 4 3 2 1

Reproduction by Pica Digital PTE Ltd, Singapore
Printed and bound by Times Offset (M) Sdn. Bhd., Malaysia

Acknowledgements

I would like to thank the following companies for supplying wire, tools, findings, ribbons and beads for the projects: 21st Century Beads, Oliver Twists,
The Scientific Wire Company, Ribbon Designs, Bond-America, Pracht and
Rayher. Special thanks also go to the editorial team at New Holland for
doing such a good job of putting the book together, and of course, to
Shona Wood for the excellent photography which shows off the projects
so beautifully.

Disclaimer

Contents

 Projects

Introduction

Wire is one of the cheapest craft materials. It is so versatile that you can create innumerable exquisite jewellery designs with only a few basic tools. A limited range of wire that is suitable for jewellery making – usually silver and gold-plated wires with a few coloured enamelled wires – is sold in most craft and bead shops, but a much greater choice is available from mail order companies and on the internet.

All of the projects in this book are quick and easy to make, and have been graded in terms of difficulty from simple to more complicated. Even if you have never worked with wire before, with a little practice each of the projects in this book is very manageable.

You may already own such basic tools as round-nose pliers, flat-nose pliers and wire cutters, and these tools are really all you need to get started. If you wish to progress further, it is relatively inexpensive to buy a set of jewellery-making tools that will make construction of small wire projects much easier. Apart from the basics, there are many other tools on the market for wirework, all of which are great fun to try. Look out for spiral makers, which can make all sorts of spiral shapes; wire jigs, to bend wire easily into shapes; and the Wyr Knittr, which makes neat wire tubes.

Wirework is a potentially addictive craft as it is so versatile, and the possibilities for design are limitless. Begin your adventure in wirework by trying the designs in this book, changing the colour of the wire and the embellishments to suit your own personal taste. Once you have made some of the projects and tried a few of the variations, you will no doubt have gained the confidence to create a few unique designs of your own.

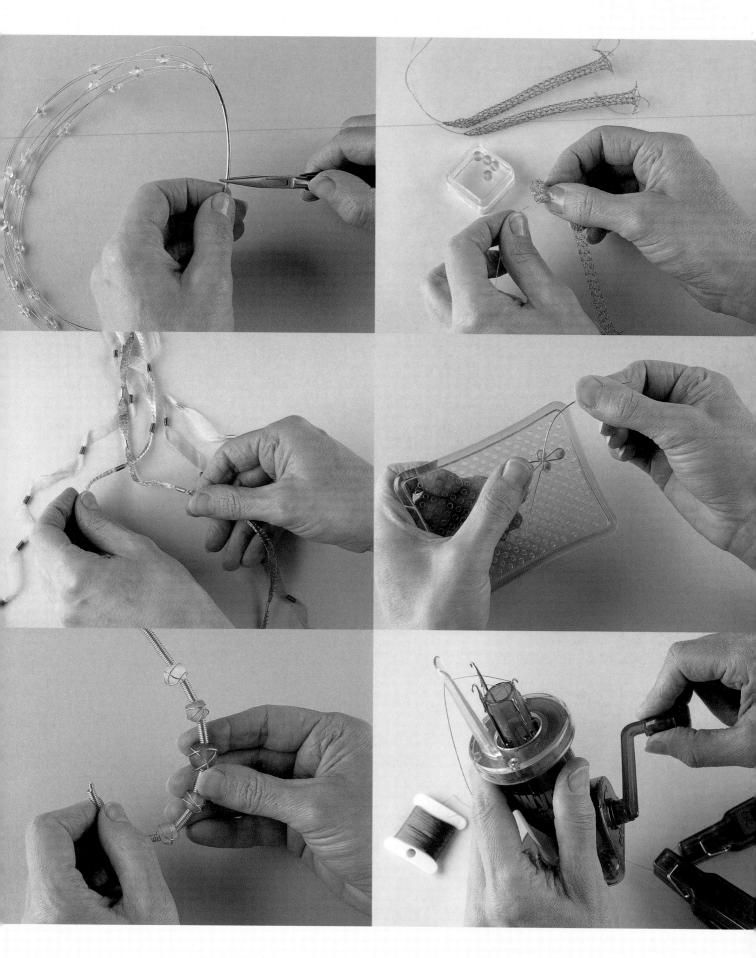

Tools

You may already have such basic tools such as wire cutters and household pliers in your toolbox, and these are enough to get you started. If, however, you plan to make the creation of wire jewellery a serious hobby, you might consider buying some of the specialist tools on the market. There are only three basic jewellery making tools: flat-nose pliers, round-nose pliers and wire cutters. These specialized tools are smaller and finer than basic wire working tools, allowing for more intricate work and overall better results.

Flat-nose pliers have pointed ends for delicacy, and flat inner surfaces that can be used to grip wire for squeezing crimps. It is important to choose a pair with smooth jaws so that the wire is less easily damaged. Heavier duty flat-nose pliers such as household pliers are useful for straightening lengths of wire before use (see page 15). If you are working with particularly soft wire, choose pliers with nylon jaws.

Round-nose pliers are one of the most useful tools for jewellery making. With round jaws that taper along their length, they are used to make jump rings, bend wire in a loop or circle, and also to make tapered coils of wire (see page 92). Choose a pair that tapers to a very fine point so that you can make very small loops for small jewellery parts.

Wire cutters have hardened steel-tempered jaws, and are available in different sizes. A small pair of wire cutters is ideal for jewellery making, as you can trim wire much more accurately on a small scale. If you hold the wire cutters with the flat side next to the jewellery you will get a flat, straight cut; if held in the other direction, the wire will be tapered. When cutting hard wires, such as memory wire, use wire cutters with hardened blades.

Wire jigs are useful for making a variety of bent wire shapes. A wire jig consists of a base plate with holes in it and an assortment of different diameter pegs to create the shape. There are several shapes of base plate, including circular, square-shaped and rectangular. Each shape has a different arrangement of holes, so you can make a wide range of patterns. Metal jigs are more expensive than wire jigs, but they allow you to bend thicker wire more easily.

French knitting tools are available with four, six or eight pins on top, allowing for the creation of different diameters of wire tubing. A Wyr Knittr is a small machine that is basically a mechanical French knitter. It has four hooks and is used with fine wire to create lengths of wire tubing that can be flattened, twisted or otherwise manipulated for different effects. Both are available from craft stores.

Spiral making tools consist of an assortment of different shapes and widths of rod that can be fitted to a winder. The user simply turns the winder and the wire wraps around the rod to create a spiral. For simple spirals you can use any round object – a knitting needle, a crochet hook, even a large darning needle – to create a range of spiral sizes. These tools are also handy for making spiral beads (see pages 24 and 54).

Paper crimpers, although meant for crimping paper, are also ideal for creating a textured wire. Simply feed the wire between the two rollers, turn the wheel and out will come a wonderfully kinky wire.

Marker pens are useful for marking wire so that you know exactly where it needs to be bent. Mark the wire with a gel ink or OHP pen before bending when you need to bend at a particular point or distance from a previous bend.

Rulers are basic but very useful tools for making jewellery. Use a ruler to measure the piece you are making so that it turns out to be the size you desire. In the case of earrings, use of a ruler is important to ensure that both earrings end up exactly the same size.

Glues that dry clear are essential for jewellery making. The two most useful glues are epoxy resin and superglue (see page 11).

Materials

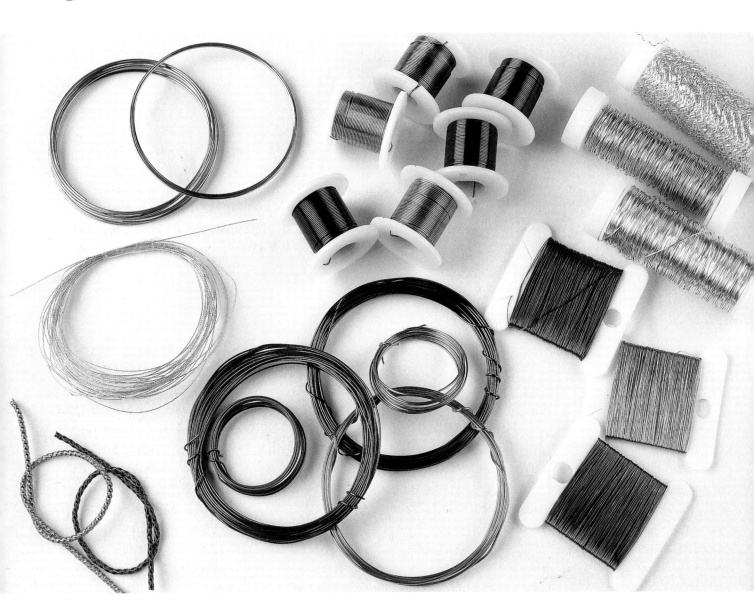

Wire

Wire can be bent, twisted and shaped to create a fantastic array of jewellery items. As well as the traditional silver and gold, there is a huge variety of different wire colours for jewellery making. Many craft and bead shops stock a small range of wires in standard sizes, but for more choice check out some of the suppliers on page 94. Before you buy wire for your project, take note of the size (gauge) that you will need and the length that is required (see chart, opposite). Many bead and craft shops sell pre-packaged sets of coordinating wire reels that look very attractive, but you may find that the length is too short to complete your project. Multi-coloured wire packs are great for trying out ideas and for inspiration, but when undertaking a project, look out for coils and reels with a reasonable quantity in the packet.

Gauges

Wire is measured in either millimetres (mm) or by the Standard Wire Gauge (swg) or (g). Wire for jewellery making generally ranges from 1 mm (19 swg) to 0.2 mm (36 swg), with about 15 different thicknesses in between. Use the conversion chart opposite as a guide.

You will see that the thicker the wire, the lower the number in standard wire gauge. The thickness

Wire gauge conversion chart

mm	swg
1	19
0.9	20
0.8	21
0.71	22
0.63	23
0.56	24
0.5	25
0.45	26
0.4	27
0.375	28
0.315	30
0.28	31
0.265	32
0.25	33
0.236	34
0.212	35
0.2	36

of wire you choose will depend on what you wish to make. For example, you should choose a wire of around 0.8 mm (21 swg) to make earrings or other such wire motifs. Finer wires may look elegant, but they can be too soft and pliable to hold their shape, especially when stored in a jewellery box together with other pieces of jewellery.

Types of wire

Wire can be made from a wide range of different materials, including copper, aluminium, steel and brass. Most jewellery making wire is made from plated or enamelled copper.

Plated wire is available in both gold and silver plates. It is an inexpensive and easy-to-use alternative to precious metal wire. This type of wire must be wrapped when stored over a long period of time, as it can tarnish if the conditions are too damp. Although not as durable as real gold or silver wire, plated wire is ideal for making everyday jewellery. If, however, you want to buy the real thing to make a special piece of jewellery, sterling silver and rolled gold wire are available from specialist suppliers (see page 94).

Enamelled wire is available in a wide range of colours, from bright and bold to subtle pastels. It is now possible to buy some very unusual colours in a range of gauges, making it much easier to make coordinated jewellery. The majority of coloured wire is enamelled copper wire, although there are now some more unusual colours known as "supa colour" craft wire, made from colour-enamelled silver-plated wire.

Crimped wire is available in 0.3 mm (30 swg) in about nine different colours. It is ideal for wrapping and creating texture in wire projects.

Tiger tail is a nylon-coated steel wire that doesn't kink in the same way as ordinary wire. It is extremely strong and is available in a range of thicknesses. The three-strand tiger tail can be knotted, but the seven-strand variety needs to be finished with crimps (see page 13).

Wax cotton is a strong cord that is an attractive alternative to wire for stringing beads. It is available in a range of colours and thicknesses. The ends must be finished with thong crimp fastenings.

Glues

There is a huge range of different glues available for craft work, although not all are suitable for jewellery making. The most important thing to check when buying glue is that it will stick the materials you are joining together. Other properties of glue that will affect your choice are the viscosity, drying time, and its clearness or opacity when dry.

Superglue is an instant bonding glue that is extremely quick to dry. It is ideal for holding beads in position along a length of wire. Gel superglue is especially effective, as it is easy to control and can be applied exactly where you want it. Ordinary liquid superglue has a tendency to run along the wire, and can look cloudy once dry. Great care must be taken when working with superglue as it will stick skin to any surface almost instantly.

Epoxy resin has two components that are mixed together to make a strong adhesive. Epoxy resins have different drying times; some take about half an hour to dry, whereas others dry in 90 seconds. Your choice of epoxy resin will thus depend on what you are using it for. Look out for the newly available clear-drying epoxy resins, as they are particularly suitable for jewellery making.

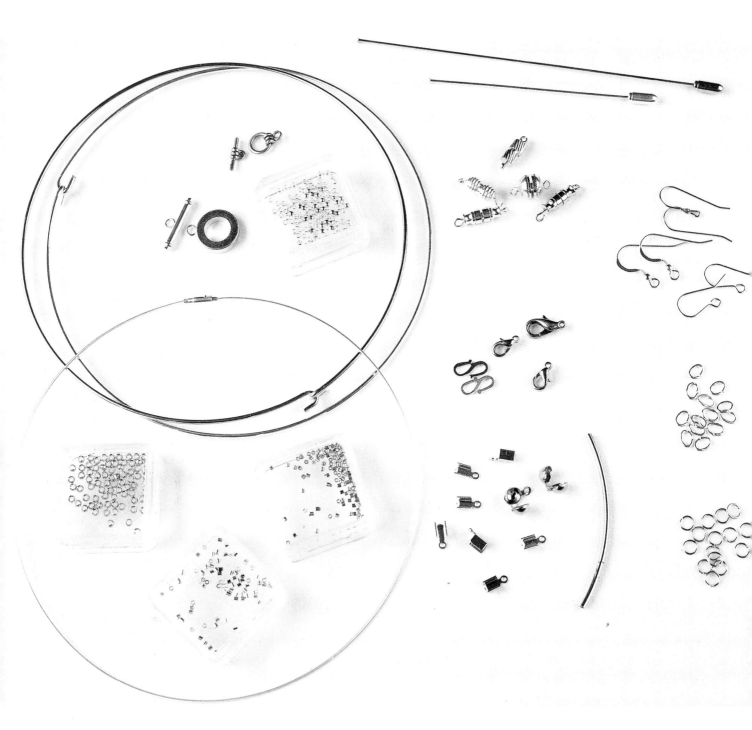

Jewellery findings

The fastenings, hooks, rings and pins used to finish or hold together pieces of jewellery are known collectively as findings. Although they are often almost invisible on the jewellery, it is important to choose findings carefully so that they enhance the finished piece. Look out for findings in sterling silver – these items are slightly more expensive than silver-plated ones, but they will make your jewellery look beautiful.

Clasps come in all shapes and sizes to suit a range of jewellery. The type of clasp you choose will depend on the item that you are making. Torpedo and barrel clasps have simple screw fastenings that are very neat and practical for use in necklaces, but are too difficult to use for bracelets. Magnetic clasps are becoming extremely popular, but check that the magnet is strong enough to hold the weight of the jewellery. Lobster clasps and toggle fastenings are suitable for both bracelets and necklaces.

Crimps are tiny silver or gold rings that can be crushed around wire to secure a bead in a particular position, to hold two pieces of wire together securely and without unsightly knots, or to secure a clasp at the end of a piece of wire. On finer wires, crimps can be made to form an attractive square that can even be a design feature of the piece. Crimps are especially useful for seven-strand tiger tail wire (see page 11).

Earring wires are used for pierced earrings. They come in an assortment of styles, such as fishhook, kidney and shepherd's crook. Although more expensive, sterling silver earring wires can make a tremendous difference to the finished look of a pair of earrings. If you are making jewellery to give as a gift, it might be wise to use a sterling silver wire in case the recipient is allergic to certain lower grade metals.

Jump rings are small circular or oval rings which have a break on one side that can be prised open by twisting with pliers. They can be used to link sections of a bracelet or necklace together. They are also useful to change the direction an earring or pendant is hanging. Jump rings can be handmade using plated wire and round-nose pliers (see page 18).

Hatpins and stick-pins are long silver- or gold-plated spikes that allow jewellery to be attached to clothing or a hat. The long spike is pinned through the item and a small protector is fitted onto the point to secure the pin.

Necklace fittings such as calotte crimps, spring ends and folding crimps are used to secure threads and wire at the end of a bracelet or necklace before the fastening is fitted.

Embellishments

It is amazing what you can do with wire when making jewellery, but it can be a bit boring to use wire alone on every piece. Embellishments such as ribbon, beads and feathers increase the design possibilities available and can add the finishing touch needed for a pair of earrings or a necklace. Embellishments should enhance rather than detract from the wirework, so choose colours and styles that co-ordinate with or match the wire colour.

Beads

Beads come in all shapes and sizes, from tiny seed beads to large decorative beads – the sheer choice can be overwhelming. You may not be able to find the exact beads used in the projects in this book, as each bead shop has a different selection, but you can easily check the size and pick your own beads to make a unique design.

Seed beads come in a range of sizes, from tiny petite beads to chunky pony beads. The most common size of seed bead is size 11, often written as 11/o or 11°. The higher the number, the smaller the bead. One of the most exciting things about seed beads is that there is a huge variety of finishes available in each colour. Be sure to ask about the durability of the finish, however, as some seed beads are not suitable for prolonged handling.

Crystals are machine-cut to produce multiple facets that catch the light. As with all beads, it pays to go for a high quality make such as Swarovski, so that you get stunning sparkle and wonderful colour effects. The most common shape of crystal is the bicone, but look out for ovals, cubes and teardrops for different effects. Crystals are available in a range of finishes, such as Aurora Borealis (AB) and lustre.

Pressed glass beads are available in a multitude of shapes because they are formed from pouring molten glass into a mould. Flowers and leaves are two of the more unusual shapes available for jewellery, although cubes, pyramids and round beads are ideal too. Pressed facetted beads are an inexpensive alternative to crystal or cut glass beads. Pressed glass beads are available in the same range of finishes as glass seed beads.

Semi-precious stones are available as round beads, carved or facetted shapes, as well as in the form of inexpensive tumble chips. These beads, which have such wonderful names as carnelian, citrine and lapis lazuli, add a touch of quality to any piece of jewellery. Some of the stones are "birthstones", and will add a little extra meaning to a gift.

Feathers have become extremely fashionable in recent years, and add a wonderful delicacy to a jewellery design. They are attached by wrapping fine wire around the quill and creating a loop at the top. Long feathers can be cut down to size and finished in the same way.

Ribbons have a wonderful tactile quality and add delicacy and softness to a piece of jewellery. Silk ribbon, specially made for ribbon embroidery, is ideal for jewellery, as it has no hard selvedge. It is available in a vast range of colours, and in widths from 2-13mm (^{1}/$_{12}$ in-^{1}/$_2$ in). Organza

ribbon is fine enough to thread through small beads and tiny spirals of wire (see page 26). Look out also for delicate metallic ribbon, which is made from a tube of knitted fine wire. It can be used flat, or it can be opened out to allow beads to be dropped inside.

Techniques

When you first look at some of the projects in this book it may be difficult to imagine how you could make such delicate wire jewellery yourself, but it is really just a matter of learning a few simple techniques. Once you have learned the basics, not only will you be able to make every design shown here; soon you will be able to adapt them to create your own unique jewellery.

Cutting wire

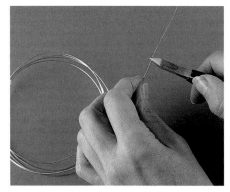

Fine wire can be cut with a pair of craft scissors, but these will get damaged if you try to cut thicker wire on a regular basis. Small wire cutters, designed for jewellery, allow you to get much closer to the work, letting you trim off the tail end accurately. If you are using memory wire, invest in a pair of special memory wire cutters.

Wire cutters have hardened steel jaws that cut through the majority of jewellery wire. Wear safety goggles when cutting long lengths in case the wire springs back into your face.

Wire cutters held in the normal way leave a bevelled edge on the end of the wire. If you hold the cutters

with the flat edge of the blade next to the work, you will be left with a straight edge that is much neater.

Straightening wire

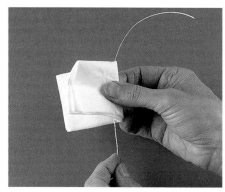

Wire is generally sold in coils and reels for practical purposes, and as a result, it has a "natural" curve when unwound. This curve can be useful – when making coils, for example – but at times a design requires a straight piece of wire. It is easier to straighten wire that is soft, but most plated or enamelled wire has a copper core that is fairly easy to stretch.

To take the gentle curve out of wire, simply fold a piece of tissue over the wire and pull it through between your finger and thumb. Exert pressure to straighten the curve.

Stretching wire

Sometimes wire gets stored or wrapped on reels badly and ends up with lots of kinks along its length. Luckily, most wire can be straightened by stretching. Fine wires can be stretched while you are working, but you will need to enlist a

friend or use a workbench and vice for thicker wires. When stretching wire it is essential to wear safety goggles and protective gloves in case the wire snaps and springs back.

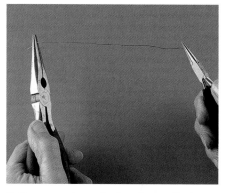

1 Grasp each end of a piece of wire with a pair of pliers and pull apart as hard as you can. It can help to exert pressure by stretching the wire across your thighs.

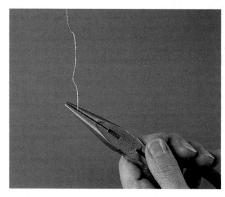

2 If the wire won't stretch by hand, use mole grips or household pliers and put one end in a vice. Pull the wire as hard as you can, using your weight to exert pressure.

Bending wire

One of the most common mistakes made when bending wire is to turn the pliers rather than the wire. When you turn the pliers, you have to turn your wrist awkwardly, so it is much better to hold the pliers still and move the wire. This way you can see exactly what you are doing and control the movement with your whole arm. Use pliers with smooth jaws so that the wire doesn't get damaged. Take care to check exactly where you are going to bend the wire, as it is likely to snap off if you try to straighten it and bend it back again. This is particularly frustrating if the piece of jewellery is almost complete, as you will need to start again.

1 Mark the wire with a permanent marker before bending if you need to bend at a particular point or distance from a previous bend.

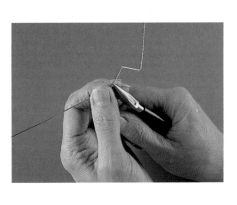

2 Grasp the wire so that you can just see the mark at the edge of the pliers and bend the wire up with your thumb.

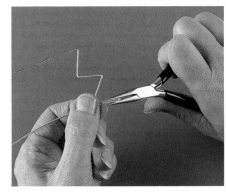

3 To make a sharp point, pinch the bent wire edges together and then open out and straighten with flat-nose pliers.

Turning a loop

One of the most common techniques used in jewellery making – turning a loop – is easy using a pair of round-nose pliers. Remember that it is easier to bend the wire itself than to turn the pliers. Loops are made either to allow a piece of wirework to be attached to an earring wire or other piece of jewellery, or to begin making a coil. As the jaws on round-nose pliers are tapered, the size of the loop will depend on where you hold the wire. For small loops, hold the wire close to the tip of the pliers.

Making a loop to finish a piece of jewellery

1 Grasp the wire close to the work with the wire in the right place for the particular size of loop you require. Hold the pliers steady and bend the wire around them with your other hand. A better result is achieved if

you hold the wire quite far down its length while bending.

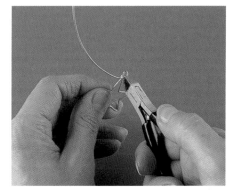

2 Snip the tail off where it begins to cross the other wire. To achieve a straight end on the wire, cut with the flat side of the cutters facing away from the tail.

Making a loop at the beginning of a piece of wire

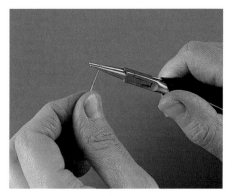

1 Cut the end of the wire so that it has a straight edge, and then hold this end in a pair of round-nose pliers so that the wire is flush with the edge of the jaws.

1 Make a loop on the end of the wire with round-nose pliers. Turn the pliers around in the loop. Hold the wire further up the tail and bend it gently around the loop.

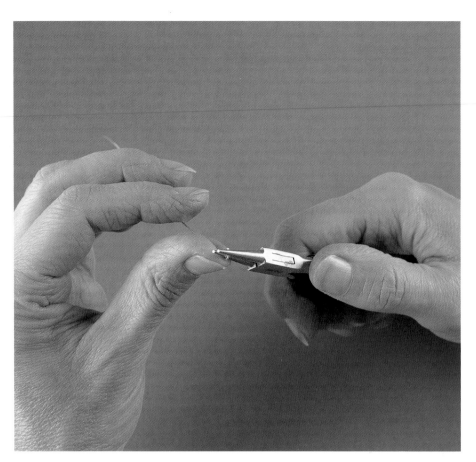

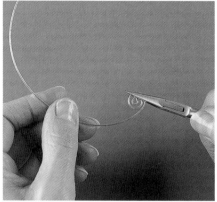

2 Change to flat-nose pliers and hold the coil between the jaws. Continue to bend the wire gently, keeping the curve soft. Holding the wire at least 2.5 cm (1 in) away from the coil helps to prevent kinks.

2 Holding the pliers still, wind the wire around the pliers with your other hand until the wire touches the end.

Making a coil

Coils are decorative elements that can be used to great effect in wire jewellery. Tight coils are the easiest to make as the wire is simply wound around so that each turn touches the last. Open coils take a little more practice, especially if you are trying to make several the same size and shape for a piece of jewellery.

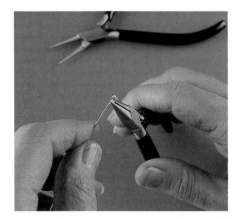

3 To make an eyepin, insert the tip of flat-nose pliers in the loop so that the jaws are touching the cut end. Bend the wire tail back slightly until it is straight.

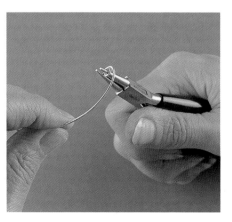

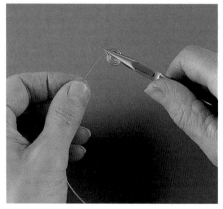

3 If you want a tight coil, hold the wire tail much closer to the loop and wind the wire so that it is tight against the previous coil. As you move the coil around, the coil shape is held flat with the pliers.

Making a spiral

Spirals are simply made by wrapping wire around a rod or similar object. You can buy tools to help you make square, round or triangular spirals, as well as unusual spiral beads. When you are making a spiral, check that the inside diameter is large enough to accommodate the cord, ribbon or wire that will go through the middle. Spirals can be closely packed or pulled open for different effects. You can also thread beads onto the wire before winding it to make unusual, sparkly spirals.

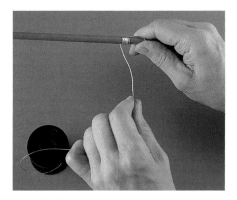

1 Hold the wire against the rod with your thumb, leaving a short tail for leverage. With your other hand, wind the wire around the rod so that the wires touch each other to form a tight spiral.

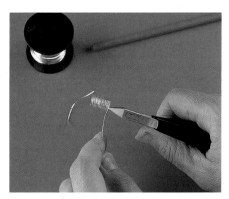

2 Count the turns you have made so that if you need to make another

spiral, it will be the same length as the first one. Slide the spiral off the rod and snip the tails off close to the end.

Using a jump ring

Jump rings are extremely useful jewellery findings. You can make your own by cutting loops made with

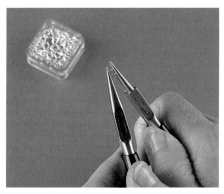

round-nose pliers, or from opened out springs. Ready-made jump rings can be round or oval and come in a range of sizes. To open a jump ring, always use a twisting action that creates a gap rather than pulling the ends apart, as this will destroy the shape of the ring.

1 Hold the ring with two pairs of pliers (two pairs of flat-nose pliers is the ideal solution, otherwise use your round-nose pliers). Twist one pair of pliers back slightly to create a gap.

2 Slip the earring or wire piece into the ring and then, using two pairs of pliers, bend in the opposite direction to close the gap.

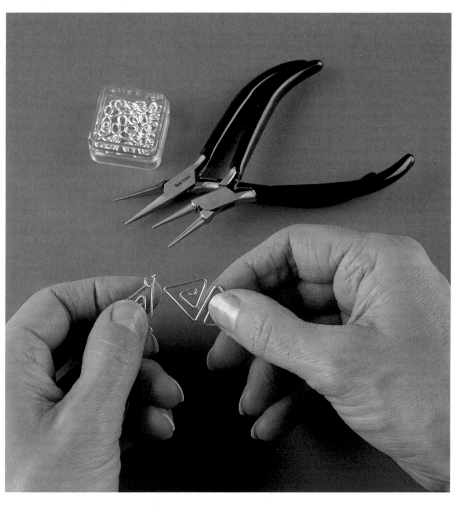

Attaching earring wires

Earring wires generally have a small loop at the end to hang the earring from. The loop is opened in a similar way to a jump ring. The correct opening and closing technique shown here preserves the shape of the loop. If you pull open the ring, it is very difficult to get it back into a neat circle.

Hold the earring wire in one hand and the loop with a pair of flat-nose pliers in the other. Twist the pliers back to open the ring. Fit the earring in the ring and close the loop by reversing the action.

Crimping

Crimping is simply a way of securing a bead, wire or thread at a particular point. Crimps are small tubular or doughnut-shaped pieces of wire that can be threaded onto wire and pinched with pliers. You can buy special crimping pliers, but flat-nose pliers do a reasonable job.

1 To secure a single length of wire on to a fastening, thread a crimp on to the wire and take the wire through the ring. Feed the end back through the crimp, crush with the tips of flat-nose pliers and trim off the end.

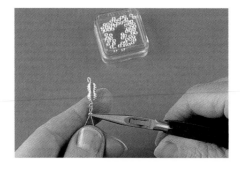

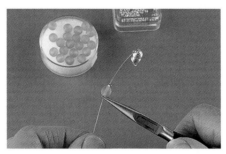

2 To secure a bead in a particular position on a length of wire or thread, you will need two crimps. Slide the bead, with the two crimps on either side of the bead, to the desired position, then use the pliers to crush the crimps.

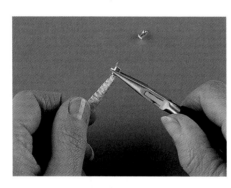

3 Crimp fastenings and thong ends work in a similar way. Trim the thread, ribbon or wire to the correct length. Lay the ends inside the fastening and squeeze the sides together with flat-nose pliers.

French Knitting

Some of the projects in this book use a tool called a Wyr Knittr to make tubes of knitted wire that look like rat's tails (see page 8). While the Wyr Knittr makes tubes mechanically, the French knitter lets you make them manually. French knitters can be bought with four, six or eight pins for knitting a range of tubing widths. The wire is fed down through the centre hole and weighted at the end with a heavy object such as a DIY plumb line. The tube is then finished in the same way as with a Wyr Knittr (see "Twisted knitted bracelet", page 32).

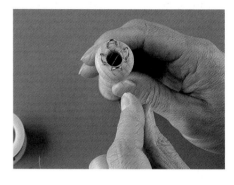

1 To cast on, wind the wire around the first pin so that the wire crosses over itself on the inside on its way to the next pin. Continue around the remaining pins, crossing the wire on the inside each time.

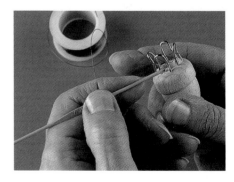

2 To knit a row, wrap the wire around the pins so that it lies above the previous stitches. Hook under the lower stitch with a crochet hook and lift it over the top stitch and the pin. Repeat on the next three pins. Wrap the wire again to begin the next row.

Eye pin earrings

A straight piece of wire with a loop at one end, the eye pin is used often in jewellery making. Eye pins are available ready-made in gold and silver, or you can make your own using coloured wire to create simple but exciting earrings.

"Choose a coloured wire that matches the different metallic colours lining the holes in these gorgeous firepolish crystals."

You will need

Materials

- 60 cm (24 in) of 0.7 mm (22 swg) pink wire
- 2 m (2 yds) of 0.4 mm (27 swg) silver-plated wire
- Two silver-plated earring wires
- Six 8 mm (5/16 in) pink-lined firepolish crystals

Tools

- Flat-nose pliers
- Household pliers
- Safety goggles
- Round-nose pliers
- Wire cutters

1 Cut six 10 cm (4 in) lengths of pink wire. Stretch each length of wire in turn to straighten it. To do this, hold each end with a pair of pliers and pull apart as hard as you can. Wear safety goggles in case the wire snaps. Snip off the bent ends of each piece of wire.

2 Using a pair of round-nose pliers, grasp a length of wire so that the end is flush with the edge of the pliers and bend the wire around using the thumb of your other hand. Change to flat-nose pliers and insert the points into the ring. Bend the tail end back slightly until the ring is straight. Repeat with the other five pieces of wire.

Helpful hint
Round-nose pliers are tapered, making it possible to create a range of different size "eyes". Make sure you hold the wire in the same place every time so that each eye is the same size.

3 Cut six 5 cm (2 in) lengths of silver-plated wire. Pick up a crystal on the end of a prepared pink wire and feed the silver-plated wire down the middle of the bead beside the pink wire. Hold the two wires with flat-nose pliers below the bead so that the bead is about 4.5 cm (1³/₄ in) from the eye.

4 Wind the silver-plated wire coming out of the top of the bead around the pink wire three or four times. Move the pliers to hold the spiral you have just made and wind the silver-plated wire at the other side of the bead in the opposite direction a few times.

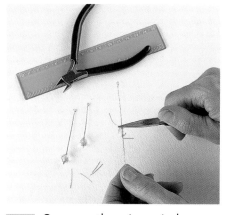

5 Squeeze the wire spirals on either side of the bead to flatten and secure them on the pink wire. Trim the ends off the silver wires and snip the pink wire end below the spiral. Make another eye pin and bead the same length, and then two which measure 4 cm (1¹/₂ in) from eye to bead and two more that measure 3.5 cm (1³/₈ in) from eye to bead.

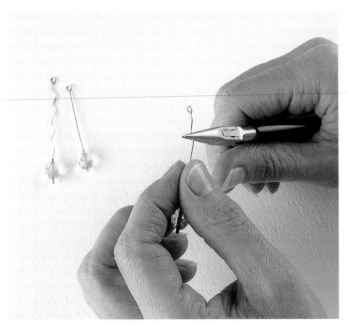

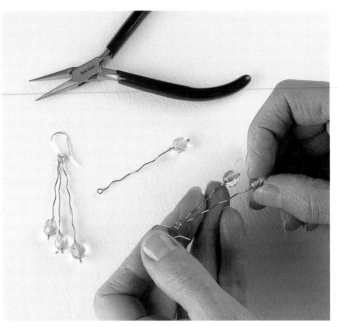

6 Grasp the pink wires just below the eye with a pair of flat-nose pliers and bend the wire back slightly. Move the pliers down below the bend and then bend the wire in the opposite direction. Continue down to the end of the wire, bending every 5 mm (¼ in). Bend each pink wire in turn.

7 Open the ring on an earring wire. Insert the three completed wires, beginning with the shortest one and finishing with the longest. Close the ring and make the second earring in the same way.

Variation

Crimped eye pin earrings

A paper crimper can be used to crimp wire as well. To make these stunningly simple earrings, cut two 6 cm (2½ in) straight eye pins using 0.7 mm (22 swg) wire. Feed the straight end into the crimper and turn the handle until the eye reaches the rollers. Release the rollers and lift out the crimped wire. Crimp the second wire in the same way. Flatten the end of the wire with flat-nose pliers and attach the bead in the same way as in the main project. Fit each earring onto an earring wire. For a more classic, formal look, leave the eye pin wires straight and attach the beads.

Spiral necklace

It is very exciting when a new product enters the market, as all of a sudden a fresh, original design is possible. One such new and exciting material is metallic ribbon. Here the ribbon adds weight to the delicate necklace and helps the lighter organdie ribbon hang nicely.

"Everyone has their own preferred colour scheme, so choose a shade of organdie ribbon, metallic ribbon and coloured wire to match your favourite outfit."

You will need

Materials

- 56 cm (22 in) of 9 mm (³⁄₈ in) organdie ribbon in fuchsia, pale pink and lilac
- 56 cm (22 in) of 7 mm (³⁄₁₆ in) metallic knitted ribbon in pink and silver
- 1 m (1 yd) of 0.5 mm (25 swg) wire in fuchsia, lilac and silver
- 1 m (1 yd) of 0.7 mm (22 swg) silver-plated wire
- 50 cm (20 in) of 0.2 mm (36 swg) silver-plated wire

- Necklace hook fastening
- Fine thread or wire

Tools

- Fine knitting needle or crochet hook
- Wire cutters
- Scissors
- Size 24 tapestry needle
- Size 10 (US size 3) knitting needle
- Flat-nose pliers

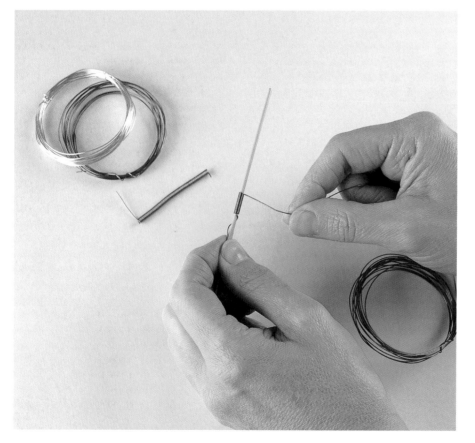

1 Hold the end of the fuchsia wire against the crochet hook and wind it around the hook to create a tightly packed spiral about 5 cm (2 in) long. Remove from the crochet hook. Make a second length in fuchsia, two in silver and one in lilac.

★☆☆ **Skill level**   🕐 **1-2 hours**   **Techniques:** *Cutting wire p.15, Making a spiral p.18, Crimping p.19*

2 Snip the tail ends off one of the fuchsia spirals and then slide your nail between the coils every 5 mm (¼ in). Pull slightly apart to create about eight short spiral lengths. Snip the stretched wire close to the end of each tightly packed section to make spiral beads. Repeat the process with the other wire spirals.

Helpful hint
Use the flat side of the wire cutters against the spiral when you are cutting off the end so the wire is trimmed as close to the spiral bead as possible.

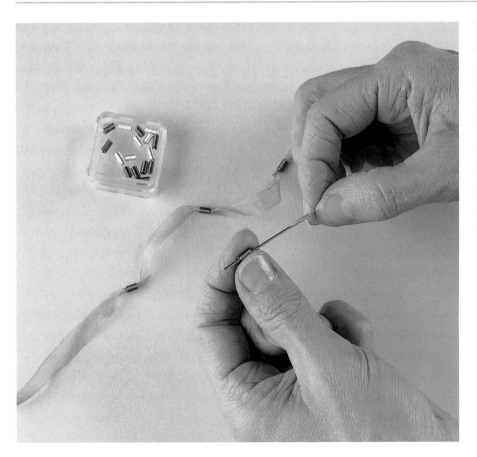

3 Thread the tapestry needle with the fuchsia organdie ribbon and pick up eight fuchsia spirals, spacing them down the length. Thread the remaining fuchsia spirals onto the metallic ribbon, the lilac spirals onto the lilac organdie ribbon and the silver spirals onto the pale pink organdie ribbon and the silver metallic ribbon.

4 To make a crimp fastening, take the 0.7 mm (22 swg) silver-plated wire and wind it around a size 10 (US size 3) knitting needle to make a tight spiral about 7 mm (⁵⁄₁₆ in) long. Snip off the ends close to the spiral, then bend out the last ring at one end to complete. Make a second fastening in the same way.

5 Layer the organdie and metallic ribbons together, then wind a piece of fine wire or thread around the end a couple of times to secure and trim them off. Tuck the bound end of the necklace into the crimp fastening you have made and squeeze the end ring with pliers to clamp the ribbons.

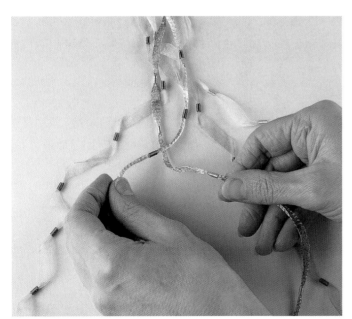

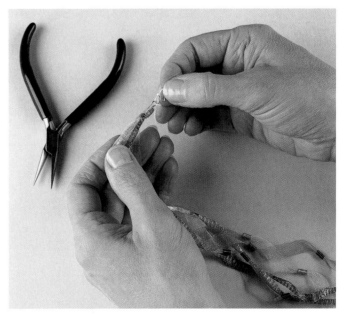

6 Tape the crimp fastening to the work surface. Loosely weave the ribbons together by simply weaving the right-hand ribbon across the other ribbons diagonally, and then weaving the new right-hand ribbon across, and so on. Continue until the necklace is completely woven.

7 Bind the ribbons together with fine thread or wire and fit the second crimp fastening. Rearrange the spirals along the lengths of ribbon until an even result is achieved. Open one crimp ring to insert the necklace hook fastening and close up again with flat-nose pliers.

Interlinked wire bracelet

Enamelled copper wire is ideal for this project as it is soft enough to bend easily and comes in a wide range of colours. Although most seed beads are size 11/00 or 12/00, in order to make this pretty bracelet you will need to ask for size 9/00 beads because the holes must be large enough to feed two pieces of wire through.

"Whichever colour wire you decide to use for your bracelet, choose one colour of seed bead to match and a lighter colour to highlight the design."

You will need

Materials

- 2.5 m (2³/₄ yds) of 0.315 mm (30 swg) turquoise wire
- Sterling silver crimp hook fastening
- About 70 each of size 9/00 pearl and aqua seed beads
- Masking tape

Tools

- Wire cutters
- Flat-nose pliers
- Tape measure

1 Cut four 60 cm (23½ in) lengths of turquoise wire. Lay them side by side on the work surface and tape across the end. Pick up three aqua seed beads on one of the outside lengths of wire. Take the wire on the other side and feed it through the three beads in the opposite direction. Pull the wires gently until the beads are sitting close to the tape.

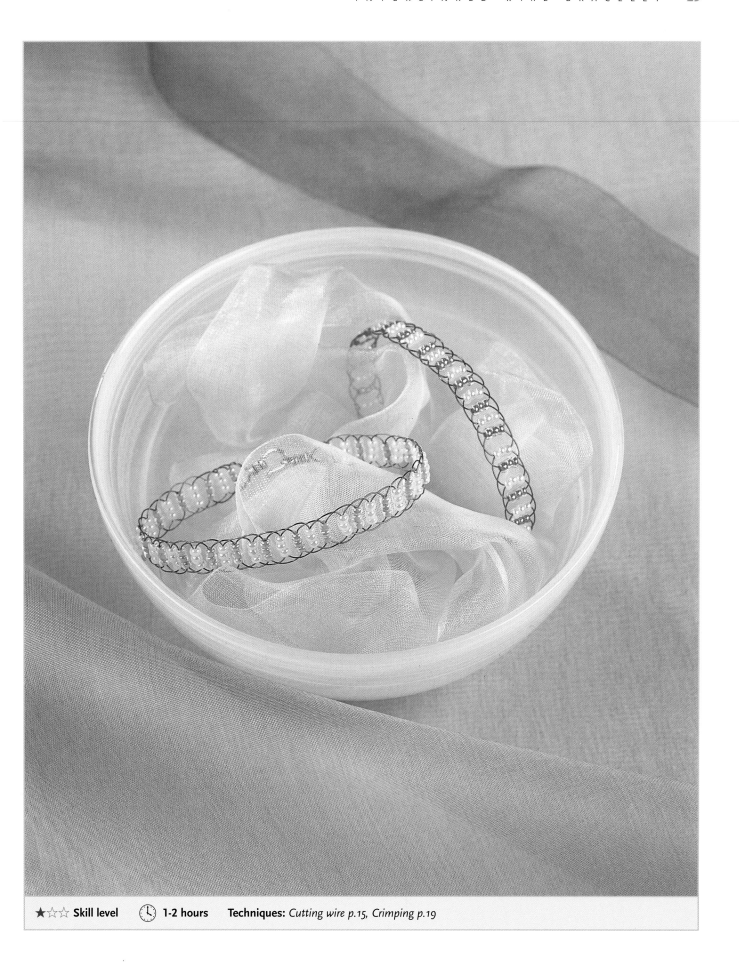

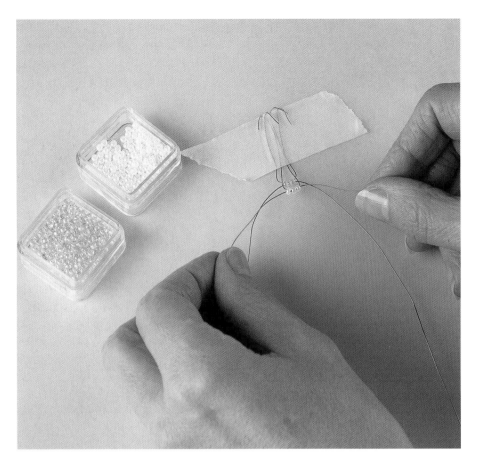

2 Bring the two remaining wires to the front. Thread three pearl seed beads onto one of the wires and feed the last wire through these seed beads in the opposite direction. Pull the wires gently until the seed beads are sitting about 3 mm (⅛ in) from the previous beads.

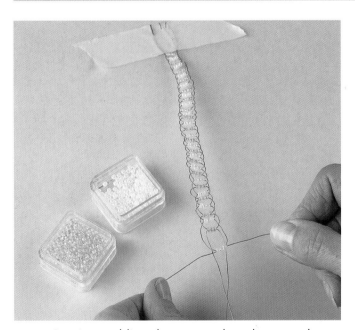

3 Continue adding three aqua then three pearl seed beads alternately, always bringing the wire that you are working with to the front of the work before you add the beads, so that the wires interlink. From now on the wires will make a soft semi-circle shape on each side.

4 Continue until the bracelet is the length required (approximately 21 rows of each colour). To find the right length for your wrist, measure your wrist with a tape measure. This tight measurement is the length from the top set of beads to the bottom set. It allows for the bracelet fastening and for finishing off, so that the bracelet will be comfortably loose when finished. Twist the pairs of wires together for 5 mm (¼ in), then twist the two twisted wires together to form a triangle at each end of the bracelet. Snip the wires off, leaving 3-4 mm (⅛-³⁄₁₆ in) to tuck inside the fastening.

5 Insert the wires into the fastening and close the crimp with the tips of flat-nose pliers. Finish the bracelet at the other end in the same way. Fit the other fastening so that it is facing in the right direction to allow the hook to link into the eye.

Helpful hint
Crimp fastenings are a neat way of finishing off this type of bracelet. If you would like to use a different fastening, however, make sure it is fitted properly before you snip off any excess wire.

Variation

Pink interlinked bracelet

This delightful bracelet was made using a vibrant pink wire, but it could have been made using any colour of wire and any combination of bead colours. Choose a bead colour that matches your wire colour, or, for a completely different effect, choose one that boldly contrasts with it.

Twisted knitted bracelet

The gorgeous texture of this wire bracelet is made by twisting two or more knitted tubes of wire together. You can make the wire tubes using a French knitting tool, or you can make them using the mechanized Wyr Knittr, which will make the tubing much more quickly.

"Any small beads can be used to decorate this gorgeous bracelet, but Swarovski crystals have a wonderful sparkle that shows off the texture of the wire beautifully."

You will need

Materials

- 10 m (10 yds) of 0.315 mm (30 swg) silver-plated wire
- 2 m (2 yds) of 0.2 mm (36 swg) silver-plated wire
- Approximately 10 each of 3 mm (1/8 in) Swarovski crystals in pale blue and deep blue
- Approximately 10 4 mm (1/6 in) Swarovski crystals in deep blue
- Sterling silver toggle fastening

Tools

- Wyr Knittr or four-pin French knitting tool
- Wire cutters

1 Make a large loop on the end of the 0.315 mm (30 swg) silver-plated wire as it comes off the reel. Feed it down through the Wyr Knittr, and attach a weight peg. Feed the other end over the wire guide and hold it against the side of the tool. Let the weight peg hang loose and turn the handle to catch the first hook. To cast on, lift the wire over the second hook, catch it in the third hook and lift it over the last hook. For casting on a French knitter, see page 19.

Helpful hint
When using the Wyr Knittr make sure that the loop drops down below the latch on the hook as it reaches its highest point so that the next stitch can form.

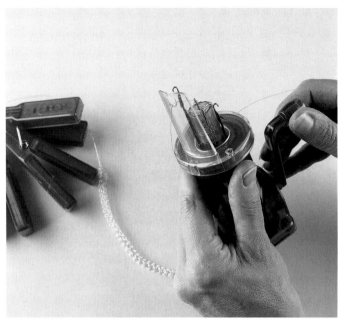

2 Continue turning the handle to catch the wire in each hook in turn to complete the casting on. Attach two more weight pegs onto the end of the tail loop. Continue turning the handle, letting the weights hang loose so that the tail is pulled down. It may help to tug the tail gently from time to time.

3 Keep turning the handle until the knitted tube measures 36 cm (14 in) from the top of the Wyr Knittr to the end. Snip the wire as it goes through the guide and, keeping the weight hanging loose, turn the handle a few times to release the knitted tube.

4 Feed the end of the wire through each loop in turn and then pull up tight. Fold the tube in half and tie a 10 cm (4 in) length of 0.315 mm (30 swg) silver-plated wire into the fold.

5 Flatten the folded knitted tube between your finger and thumb. Hold the flattened tubes between your finger and thumb of both hands. Turn your hands in opposite directions to twist the knitted tube. Move your hand along to the next bit of tube and twist again. Continue until it is all twisted.

6 Attach the finer silver-plated wire to one end of the twisted wire bracelet. Pick up a crystal and feed the wire back through the bracelet.

7 Continue adding the three different crystals in a random order until the bracelet is covered in beads. Loop the wire through the hole of the toggle fastening a couple of times, then wrap it around below the fastening to secure. Feed the ends through the bracelet and snip off.

Variation

Delicate twisted bracelet

A great variety of beautiful designs is possible using knitted tubing. A single length of knitted tube can be used to make a delicate bracelet. The bracelet shown here was made by simply twisting three or more lengths together and decorating with beads. Another option is to make earrings, as shown on page 33, that would be an ideal gift for a bridesmaid. Simply feed the wire ends of a 7 cm (3 in) length of beaded, twisted tube into the ring of an earring wire and tie off the ends. Make another earring to match.

Tiger tail necklace

Tiger tail is a steel wire with a nylon coating that prevents it from kinking in the same way as normal wire. The wire bends in a soft curve, making it ideal for creating simple necklaces. Choose classic silver wire or one of the other subtle colours available.

"The simple tube fastening used in this project is made specially for tiger tail necklaces, but other types of crimp fastenings will work equally well."

You will need

Materials
- 3 m (3¼ yds) of seven-strand silver tiger tail
- Silver-plated tubular necklace crimp fastening
- 26 pale pink pyramid crystals
- 2 g size 9/00 crystal seed beads
- Gel superglue
- Masking tape

Tools
- Wire cutters
- Flat-nose pliers
- Ruler

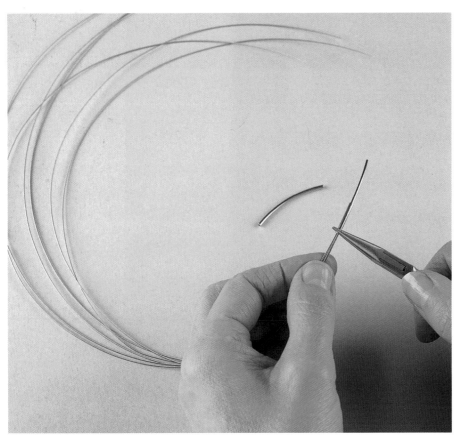

1 Cut six 45 cm (18 in) lengths of tiger tail. Feed the ends into one side of the necklace crimp fastening and squeeze the end of the fastening with flat-nose pliers to secure.

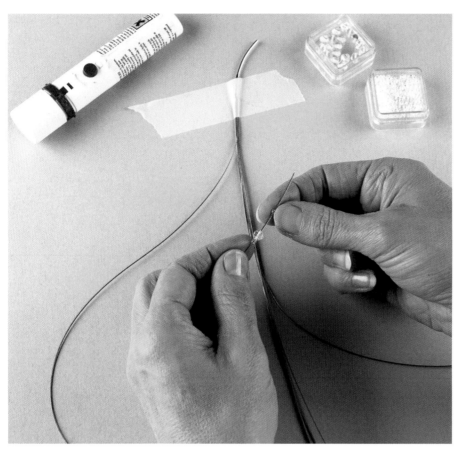

2 Tape the fastening to the work surface and spread the wires out. Pick up one seed bead, a pyramid crystal and another seed bead. Push them up to the top of the strand. Stick the top seed bead in position with a drop of glue, push the pyramid up to meet it and then stick the other seed bead on the other side.

Helpful hint
If you can find it, gel superglue is the best glue to stick the beads into position, as it is easy to control the quantity applied.

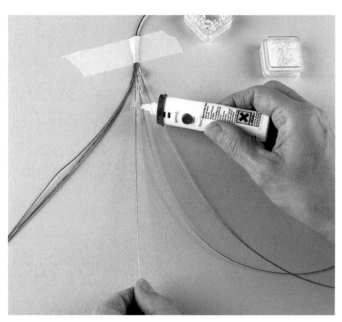

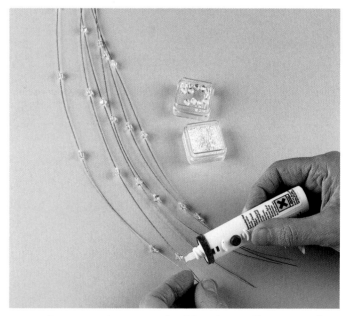

3 Pick up the same three beads on the next strand along and push up until they are about 1 cm (½ in) below the first set. Stick the two seed beads on either side of the pyramid. Work across from strand to strand, picking up three beads each time and sticking them 1 cm (½ in) down from the previous set.

4 Once you have attached beads to all six strands, begin again on the first strand, sticking the beads 1 cm (½ in) below the level of the last set of beads added. Continue adding beads in this way until you are about 2.5 cm (1 in) from the ends of the wires.

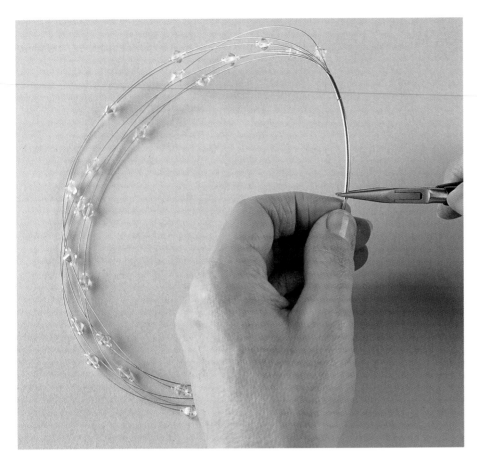

5 Hold the wires together and check that the beaded wires hang attractively, adjusting them if necessary. Feed the ends of the tiger tail into the other end of the necklace fastening. Close the fastening and then squeeze the crimp end to close so that both flat edges are facing in the same direction.

Variation

Tiger tail earrings

Cut a 12 cm (4³/₄ in) length of tiger tail. Feed it through the ring on the earring wire and push both ends through a 2.5 mm crimp. Hold the cut ends together and slide the crimp up the tiger tail. Allow the tiger tail ends to cross over as you get near the earring wire. Squeeze the crimp with flat-nose pliers so that the flat surface is at the front of the earring and the tiger tail ends splay out to each side. Pick up a seed bead, a pyramid crystal and another seed bead with one end of the tiger tail. Apply a drop of glue 3.5 cm (1³/₈ in) from the crimp and slide the seed bead up to stick. Push the crystal up and stick the second seed bead on the other side. Stick beads on the other strand to match. When the glue has dried, snip off the excess tiger tail. Make a second earring to match.

Knitted necklace

This "tube within a tube" design is a simple idea that has been given a contemporary slant with the addition of these beautiful frosted beads. The beads have a much larger hole than most, so that the tube can slide easily through the centre.

"A magnetic fastening is ideal for lightweight pieces of jewellery such as this necklace. Not only does it look stylish, it also puts an end to the need to fiddle with screw fastenings or hooks behind the wearer's neck."

You will need

Materials

- 10 m (10 yds) of 0.2 mm (36 swg) pink wire
- 10 m (10 yds) of 0.2 mm (36 swg) burgundy wire
- Three round pink frosted beads with 5 mm (¼ in) centre hole
- Four 1 cm (⅝ in) doughnut-shaped pink frosted beads with 5 mm (¼ in) centre hole
- Necklace fastening (any kind, but metallic if possible)
- Gel superglue

Tools

- Wyr Knittr or French knitting tool
- Wire cutters
- Long needle or bodkin
- Flat-nose pliers
- Ruler

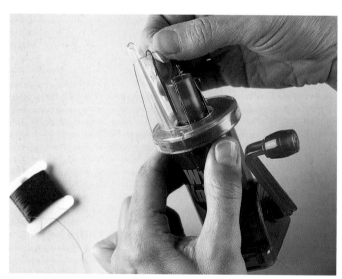

1 Make a large loop on the end of the 0.2 mm (36 swg) pink wire as it comes off the reel. Feed it down through the Wyr Knittr and attach a weight peg. Feed the other end over the wire guide and hold it against the side of the tool. Let the weight peg hang loose and turn the handle to catch the first hook. To cast on, lift the wire over the second hook, catch it in the third hook and lift it over the last hook.

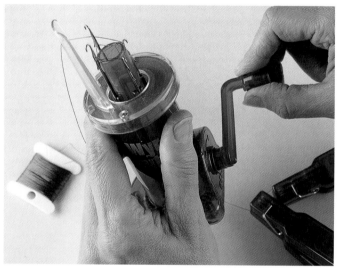

2 Continue turning the handle to catch the wire in each hook in turn to complete the casting on. Attach one more weight peg onto the end of the tail loop. Turn the handle, letting the weights hang loose so that the tail is pulled down. On this gauge of wire the knitted tube should move through easily, but if not, it can help to tug the tail gently from time to time. To cast on using a French knitting tool, see page 19.

★☆☆ **Skill level**   🕐 **1-2 hours**   **Technique:** *French knitting p.19*

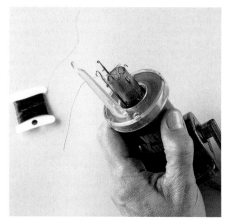

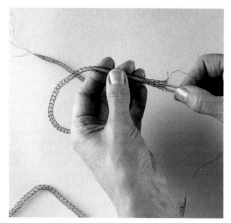

3 Keep turning the handle until the knitted tube measures 46 cm (18 in) from the top of the Wyr Knittr to the end. Snip the wire as it goes through the guide and, keeping the weight hanging loose, turn the handle a few times in order to release the knitted tube.

4 Feed the tail end of the pink wire through the loops at the end of the pink wire tube and pull up to close. Roll the pink wire tube very gently on your lap to make it slightly narrower.

5 Make a burgundy knitted tube the same length as the pink tube, but leave the end open. Thread the pink tube wire into a long needle or bodkin and twist the wire to secure. Feed the needle or bodkin up through the burgundy tube and out the hole at the top. Tie the wires together to secure.

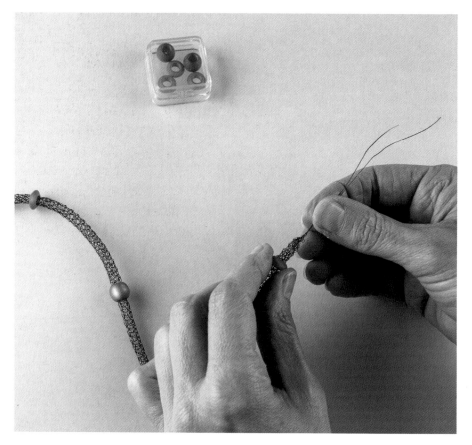

6 Close the burgundy tube at the other end by feeding the tail through the loops. Tie the pink and burgundy wires together. Slide a doughnut bead, then a round bead over the tube, and repeat until there are four doughnut beads and three round beads on the wire tube.

Helpful hint
If you decide to use different beads than the ones shown here, make sure their holes are large enough to allow the tube to slide easily through their centres.

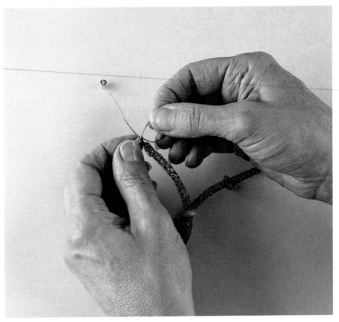

7 Move the beads along the wire tube so that they are evenly spaced, with a round bead in the centre. One at a time, move each bead slightly to one side, apply a few drops of superglue and slide the bead back.

8 Pick up a necklace fastening on the end wire and wind it back through the ring once more. Twist the wire around the necklace and then feed the ends through the tube and snip off the excess wire. Attach a fastening to the other end.

Variation

Green and gold necklace

The "tube within a tube" design can be used to make a wide range of coloured necklaces and bracelets. This necklace has a gold tube inside a deep green tube, and is finished with green frosted beads and a matching gold-plated necklace fastening. For a different effect, try dropping beads into the Wyr Knittr as you knit rather than adding them onto the outside.

Bullion bracelet

Bullion is a ready-made decorative wire product that is generally used for metallic embroidery. It is sold in lengths that are rather snake-like, and if stretched, the bullion looks like a fine spring. In this project the bullion has been cut into short lengths to form metal "beads".

"Bullion is available in a range of colours, textures and widths. Choose a 2-3 mm (¹⁄₁₆-¹⁄₈ in)-wide style that will not hang too loose on the wire."

You will need

Materials

- 0.5 m (½ yd) of 0.7 mm (22 swg) silver-plated wire
- 15 cm (6 in) of 2-3 mm (¹⁄₁₆ in) silver bullion
- Silver jump ring
- Silver lobster claw clasp

Tools

- Wire cutters
- Round-nose pliers
- Flat-nose pliers
- Small scissors

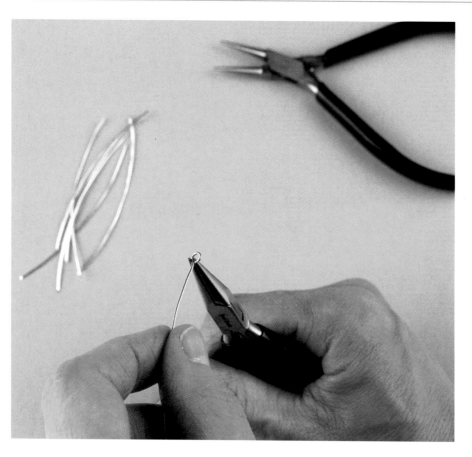

1 Cut seven 6 cm (2½ in) lengths of silver-plated wire. Using a pair of round-nose pliers, grasp a length of wire so that the end is flush with the edge of the pliers, and bend the wire around using the thumb of your other hand. Change to flat-nose pliers and insert the point into the ring. Bend the tail end back slightly until the ring is straight. Repeat with the other six pieces of wire.

★☆☆ **Skill level**   🕐 **1-1½ hours**   **Techniques:** *Cutting wire p.15, Turning a loop p.16, Using a jump ring p.18*

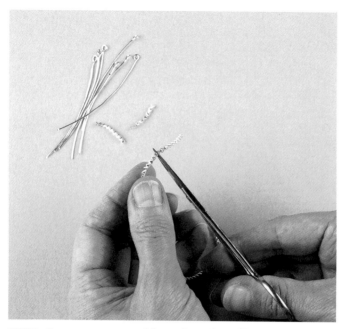

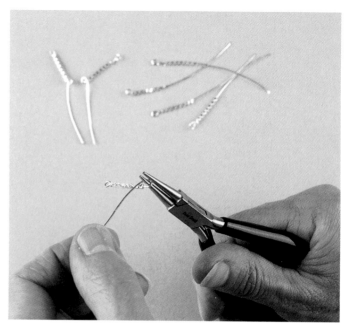

2 Cut seven 2 cm (3/4 in) lengths of bullion. You will find it easier and neater to use a small pair of scissors to cut the bullion. Slide one piece of bullion onto each piece of prepared wire.

3 Using a pair of round-nose pliers, hold the wire just above the end of the bullion. Bend the wire around the point of the pliers to create a ring. Repeat with the other six wires.

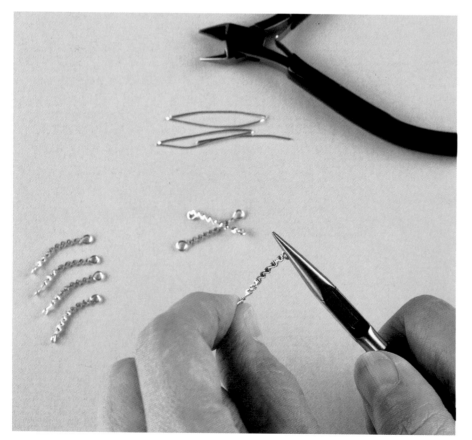

4 Snip the excess wire on each ring. Hold one ring between your finger and thumb, and the other in the flat-nose pliers. Twist the rings so that one is horizontal and the other is vertical. Bend each piece gently over your thumb to shape into a slight curve.

Helpful hint
It is better to bend the bullion links into a gentle curve once they have been completed, as the bullion will prevent the inside wire from kinking.

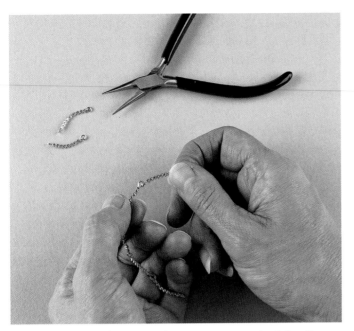

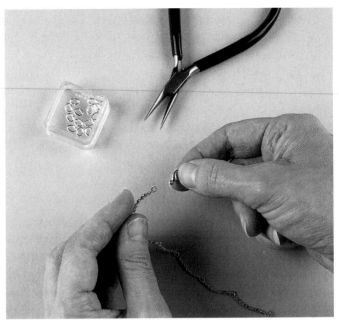

5 Open the horizontal ring at one end of the first bullion link and fit it into the vertical ring on the next bullion link. Squeeze closed. Continue adding links until they are all joined together.

6 Open one end ring and fit a silver jump ring. Open the ring at the other end and fit a lobster claw clasp to complete the bracelet.

Variation

Bead and bullion bracelet

For different options using this design technique, you can make your bracelet any length you want; you can even have two or three lengths linked into the same clasp. For a more ornate bracelet, add beads or other embellishments to the wire links before they are joined together. To make the design shown here, cut the bullion into 7 mm (⁵/₁₆ in) lengths and thread on a bead in between the two pieces. Join the bullion links as shown in the main project.

Bead and spiral bracelet

Spirals are simple to make, and can be made in a range of shapes and sizes. It is helpful to use a spiral-making tool for this bracelet, as the wire is quite thick. A spiral-making tool has a hole to secure the end of the wire and a handle to wind it, so you can easily make long lengths of spiral.

"An alternative way to make this bracelet is to use a length of round memory wire as the base, however the bracelet will sit more neatly around your wrist as an oval shape."

You will need

Materials

- 10 m (10 yds) of 0.9 mm (20 swg) lemon wire
- 10 m (10 yds) of 0.7 mm (22 swg) lemon wire
- One 12 mm (½ in) round coral frosted bead
- Two 8 mm (⁵⁄₁₆ in) round yellow frosted beads
- Two 8 mm (⁵⁄₁₆ in) round orange frosted beads
- 25 cm (10 in) of 1.5 mm (16 swg) silver-plated wire
- Gel superglue

Tools

- Spiral tool with 2 mm (¹⁄₁₂ in)-wide rod
- Wire cutters
- Ruler

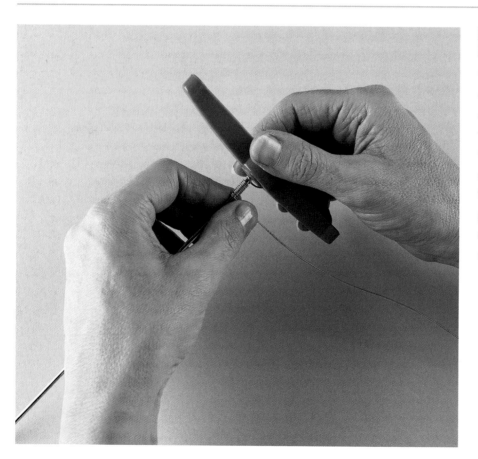

1 Fit a 2 mm (¹⁄₁₂ in) rod into the winding mechanism of the spiral tool. Feed the end of the 0.9mm (20 swg) lemon wire into one of the holes and begin to turn the winder to bend the wire around the rod. (If you turn in the wrong direction, the rod will unscrew from the winder.) Use your thumb to guide the wire so that the spiral is closely packed. Continue turning until the spiral is 15 cm (6 in) long.

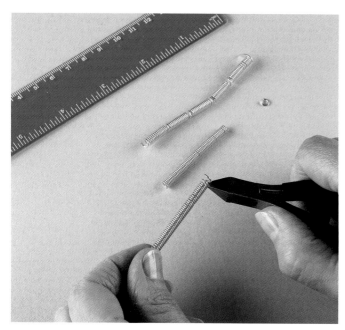

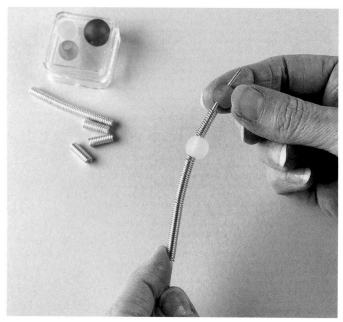

2 Remove the spiral from the rod and cut into two 4.5 cm (1³/₄ in) lengths and four 12 mm (¹/₂ in) lengths. To cut the spiral, bend at the point you want to cut and pull apart slightly. Trim the ends of the spiral neatly.

3 Cut a 25 cm (10 in) length of 1.5 mm (16 swg) silver-plated wire. Feed one of the long spirals onto the wire, then a yellow bead, a short spiral, an orange bead, a short spiral, a large coral bead, a short spiral, an orange bead, a short spiral, a yellow bead and the other long spiral.

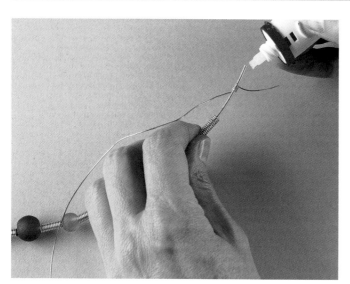

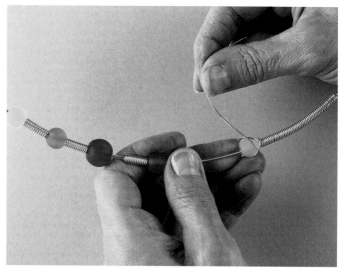

4 Cut a 75 cm (29¹/₂ in) length of 0.7 mm (22 swg) lemon wire. Wind the wire around one end of the silver-plated wire about four times. Let the spiral slide down the wire slightly, apply a few drops of superglue on the end of the silver-plated wire and carefully slide the spiral back to the end. Once the glue has dried, snip off the short end of the lemon wire.

5 Feed the long end of the lemon wire through the first spiral and out next to the yellow bead. Holding the yellow bead steady, wrap the wire around the bead several times and then feed it through the next spiral. Wrap the wire around each bead in turn and then feed through the last long spiral. You can glue the bead into position to make it easier to wrap the wire around.

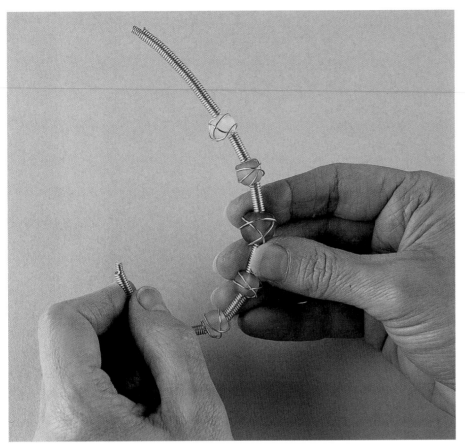

6 Apply a few drops of superglue onto the silver-plated wire at the end of the long spiral. Carefully wind the lemon wire around the silver-plated wire four times and leave to dry. Trim the lemon wire, then trim the silver-plated wire flush with the end of the spiral. Bend the bracelet into an oval shape to fit your wrist. To close the bracelet, gently push the ends together.

Helpful hint
To control the curve of the wire when shaping the bracelet, hold your thumb against the inside of the bracelet and curve the wire over it to create the oval shape.

Variation

Gold-plated torque necklace

This technique can also be used to make a matching necklace using a gold-plated torque. Make a lemon spiral with 0.9 mm (20 swg) wire that is slightly shorter than the length of the torque. Cut four 12 mm (½ in) pieces to put between the beads, as well as two longer lengths, approximately 13 cm (5 in) each. Make the necklace in the same way as the bracelet, leaving the ends of the torque jutting out from the finer spiral so that it can be fastened.

Coil and spiral earrings

These gorgeous earrings are created using three simple wire techniques: bending, coiling and wrapping. In this contemporary design, spiral beads, formed using coloured wire, are offset by simple gold-plated wire that comprises the main shape of the earrings.

"There is no need to buy special equipment to make spirals. Simply look through your work box for fine knitting needles or crochet hooks to wrap the wire around."

You will need

Materials

- 60 cm (24 in) of 0.8 mm (21 swg) gold-plated wire
- 2 m (2 yds) of 0.5 mm (25 swg) wine-coloured enamelled wire
- Two gold-plated earring hooks
- Tissue
- Two gold beads

Tools

- Wire cutters
- Flat-nose pliers
- Round-nose pliers
- Two fine crochet hooks or knitting needles, one 2 mm (size 0) and the other 1.5 mm (2.5 US steel/size 000), for wrapping
- Ruler

1 Cut a 30 cm (12 in) length of 0.8 mm (21 swg) gold-plated wire. Hold the wire in the round-nose pliers so that the end is flush with the edge of the pliers. Bend the wire around the pliers to form a ring. Move the pliers around the ring slightly, then bend the tail around the pliers again to begin forming the coil.

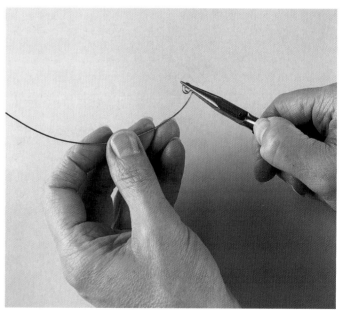

2 Change to flat-nose pliers. Hold the coil in the pliers and bend the tail gently around. Keep moving the coil around and bending the wire gently until the coil is about 7 mm (5/16 in) in diameter. Fold a tissue over the tail of the wire and pull the wire several times to take the curve out of it.

★★☆ **Skill level**   🕐 **1-2 hours**   **Techniques:** *Bending wire p. 16, Making a coil p.17, Making a spiral p.18*

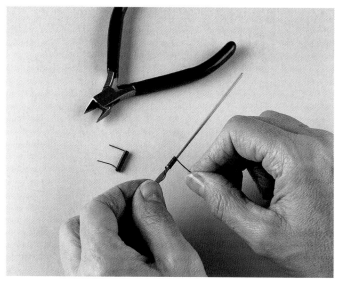

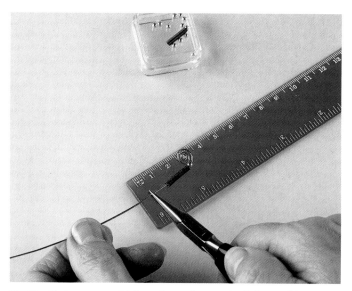

3 Wrap some of the wine-coloured wire around the handle of a 2 mm (size 0) knitting needle or crochet hook to make a spiral, ensuring that you can feed two thicknesses of the gold-plated wire through the middle. To make a spiral, wrap the wine-coloured wire around the hook or needle 25 times. Slide the spiral off the hook or needle and trim the ends.

4 Pick up a gold bead on the end of the gold wire and then feed on the wine spiral. Using the flat-nose pliers, bend the gold wire 3 cm (1⅛ in) from the top of the gold coil.

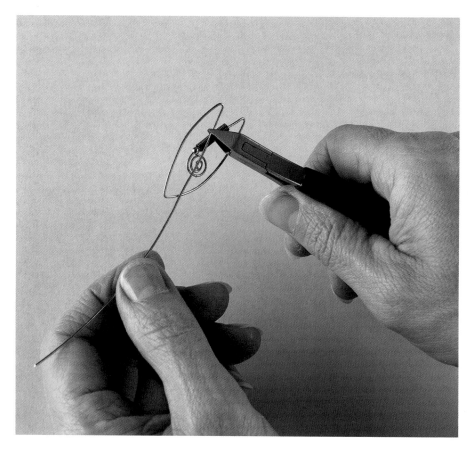

5 Bend the wire again approximately 4.5 cm (1¾ in) from the previous bend to form the top of the earring. Shape this last section into a gentle curve by running the wire between your finger and thumb. Measure 4 cm (1½ in) from the previous bend and bend the wire one last time. Shape the second side into a gentle curve. Snip the tail off 12 mm (½ in) from the last bend. Push the spiral and bead up as far as it will go and tuck the tail end into the spiral.

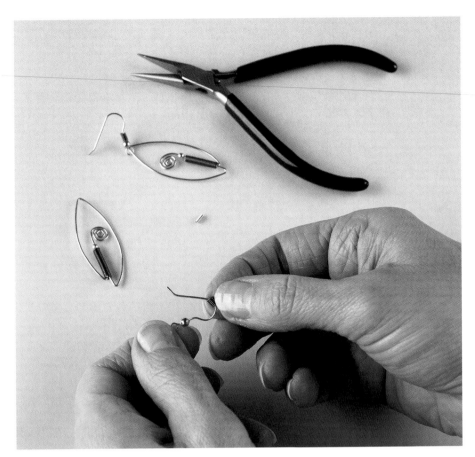

6 Slide the gold spiral off the gold-plated earring hook. Make a wine-coloured spiral to replace it by wrapping the wine-coloured wire six times around a 1.5-mm (2.5 US steel) crochet hook or a 1.5-mm (size 000) knitting needle. Snip off the ends of the spiral, then feed it onto the earring hook. Twist the ring on the earring hook open and insert the gold earring. Close the ring and make a second earring to match.

Helpful hint

When making earrings that are asymmetrical, like these ones, fit the earrings in their hooks so that the coils are facing opposite each other to make a balanced pair.

Variations

Circle earrings

Cut a 20 cm (8 in) length of 0.8 mm (21 swg) gold-plated wire. Find a sewing thread reel or similar item that is approximately 28 mm (1¼ in) in diameter. Wrap the wire around the reel to form a circle in the middle of the wire. Make a wine-coloured spiral 25 coils long (see step 3, opposite) and feed onto one end of the gold wire. Feed the other end through in the opposite direction. Trim the wire ends 3.5 cm (1³/8 in) from the edge of the spiral. Coil the ends. Fit to an earring hook. Make a earring second to match.

"S"-shaped earrings

Cut an 11 cm (4¼ in) length of 0.8 mm (21 swg) gold-plated wire and make a small coil at one end. Make a larger coil at the other end so that you have a "c"-shaped piece 32 mm (1¼ in) long. Hold the two coils, one in each hand, between your finger and thumb and twist in opposite directions, forming an "s" shape. Cut a 15 cm (6 in) length of 0.315 mm (30 swg) gold-plated wire. Pick up a gold bead, a 25-turn thin wine-coloured spiral (see step 6, above), and another gold bead. Wrap the wire around the coils and back through the beads and spirals, then wrap the ends around beside the beads and trim. Fit to an earring hook. Make a second earring to match.

Crochet necklace

Unlike the majority of beads, semi-precious tumble chips have irregular shapes, lending a piece of jewellery a wonderful individuality. Look out for wire that is sold specifically for crochet, as this type of wire is specially made so as not to snap or break easily.

"If you are making this necklace as a gift, choose semi-precious stones with special meaning, such as citrine for strength and self-confidence and carnelian for courage."

You will need

Materials

- 10 m (10 yds) of gold-plated crochet wire 0.315 mm (30 swg)
- 45 cm (18 in) length of citrine and carnelian semi-precious tumble chips
- Ball crimp end
- Gold-plated necklace fastening
- Masking tape

Tools

- Size 1.5 mm (2.5 US steel) crochet hook
- Wire cutters
- Flat-nose pliers

1 Transfer 30 carnelian stone chips onto the crochet wire. Semi-precious chips are generally sold on a ready-made necklace with two threads running through the middle. If you remove one of the fastenings and the first few chips, then pull out one of the threads about 30 chips back, you should be able to feed the wire through the chips a few at a time. Otherwise, place 30 stone chips in the palm of your hand and feed the wire into the holes in the chips, one chip at a time.

★★☆ **Skill level**   🕐 **3-4 hours**   **Techniques:** *Cutting wire p.15, Crimping p.19*

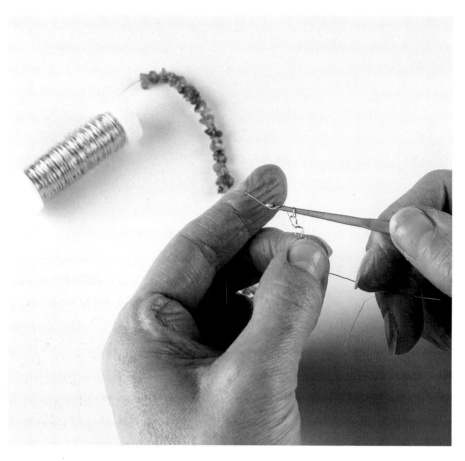

2 Make a slip knot about 10 cm (4 in) from the end of the crochet wire. Insert the crochet hook into the loop and pull it fairly tight. Work four chain stitches. To work chain, hold the hook as shown in one hand. Wrap the wire coming off the reel around the little finger of your other hand to create tension in the wire, then loop it over your index finger. To make a chain stitch, move the tip of the hook under the tensioned wire so that the wire goes across the hook. Hold on to the tail of the crochet and gently pull the wire through the loop to create a stitch.

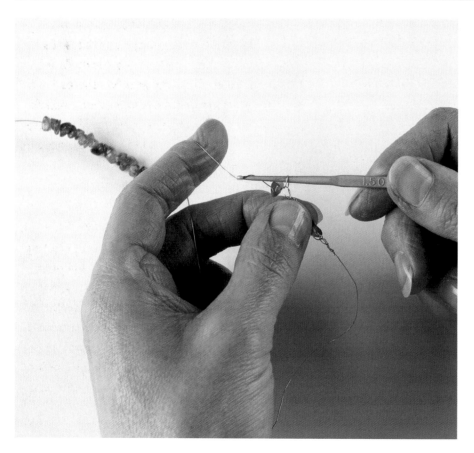

3 Once you have worked four chain stitches, bring a stone chip up to the crochet hook. Work a chain over the top of the chip. Work another four chain stitches and add another stone chip. Continue until all 30 stone chips are added, then work a final four chain stitches.

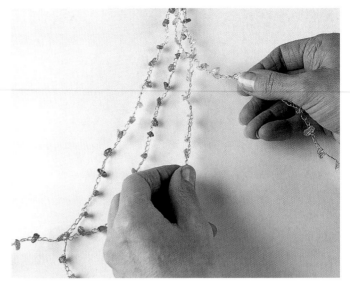

4 Trim the tail to 10 cm (4 in), feed the end through the last loop and pull tight. Make a second gold chain using carnelian chips, then two more using the citrine chips so that you have four lengths in all.

5 Tape the wires at one end onto the work surface. Loosely plait the four chains together. To do this, simply take one of the outside chains and tuck it over one chain, under the next and over the last. Continuing to work from the same side, take the new outside chain going under, over, then under this time. Continue alternating between these two steps until the necklace is plaited.

6 Feed the wires into a ball crimp end. Twist the wires together and trim to 5 mm (1/4 in). Fold the wires into half the ball crimp and close with pliers. Attach the necklace fastening and squeeze the crimp fastening with flat-nose pliers to secure.

Helpful hint

This necklace is extremely easy to make as it uses only the simplest crochet stitch. If you have never crocheted before, practise making chain stitches with a larger hook and cotton yarn until you are comfortable holding the tail and maintaining the tension to create even-sized stitches.

Wrapped star earrings

Crimped wire adds an unusual textured finish to these delicate little earrings. You can buy crimped wire in a range of colours, or try crimping your own by feeding straight wire through a paper crimper.

"To create fun, everyday earrings in this style that are less formal, simply replace the subtle silver wire with two brightly coloured contrasting wires and add sparkly delica beads."

You will need

Materials
- White scrap paper
- 32 cm (12½ in) of 0.7 mm (22 swg) silver-plated wire
- 2 m (2 yds) of 0.2 mm (36 swg) silver-plated wire
- 24 metallic delica beads (D512)
- Two silver-plated earring hooks

Tools
- Flat-nose pliers
- Round-nose pliers
- Wire cutters
- Ruler
- Black gel pen
- Paper crimper

1 Mark two lines 7 mm (⁵⁄₁₆ in) apart on a scrap of white paper. Cut a 16 cm (6¼ in) length of 0.7 mm (22 swg) silver-plated wire. Straighten the wire if it is curved or slightly kinked. Beginning 2.5 cm (1 in) from one end, make 11 marks, each 7 mm (⁵⁄₁₆ in) apart, along the wire.

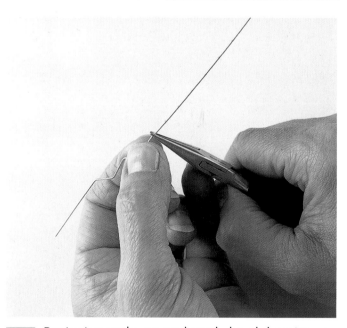

2 Beginning at the second mark, bend the wire up exactly on the line with flat-nose pliers. Bend the wire down at the next mark and so on until you end up with a zigzag pattern.

★★☆ **Skill level**   🕐 **1-2 hours**   **Techniques:** *Bending wire p.16, Turning a loop p.16, Attaching earring wires p.19*

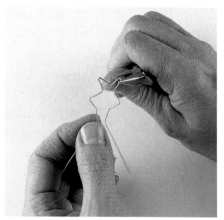

3 Bring the two ends together to see the star shape begin to form. Bend the two wires back at the last marks to create the top point. At each of the star points, pinch the wires together with flat-nose pliers and then open out to form a sharp point. Straighten the wire on each side of the point again by pressing with flat-nose pliers.

4 Form the wire back into a star shape. Bend the two top wires so that they sit next to one another above the top point of the star. Hold the star with flat-nose pliers so that the top of the star is level with the top edge of the pliers. Hold the long end of the wire and twist this around the shorter wire three times to make three tight coils. Trim off the long tail.

5 Hold the shorter wire just above the coils with the very tip of the round-nose pliers. Bend the wire around the pliers to make a small loop. Trim the end. Hold the loop in the flat-nose pliers and straighten it slightly.

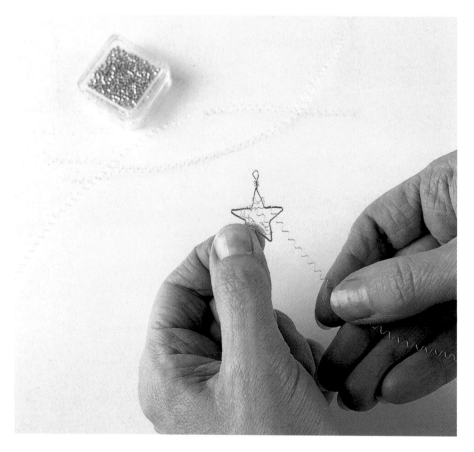

6 Cut four 30 cm (12 in) lengths of 0.2 mm (36 swg) wire and feed through a crimping machine. Secure one end of the crimped wire to the top of the star and wrap the length around and over the star to cover it. Tuck the end in. Wrap a further two lengths.

Helpful hint

If you do not have a crimping machine, you can buy ready-made crimped wire that can be used straight off the reel. For a less textured effect, use a wire that has not been crimped.

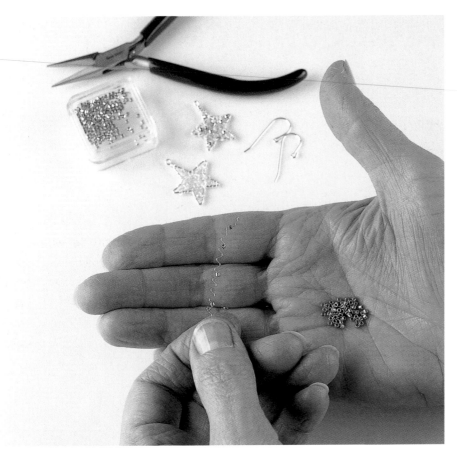

7 Pick up 12 delica beads on the last piece of wire. Let the beads fall down so that they're spaced out along the wire. Wrap this last piece of wire around the star so that the beads decorate one side only. Twist open the ring on an earring fastening and insert the star. Close the ring. Make a second earring to match.

Variation

Star necklace

Use the star motif once again to make a stunning necklace to match your earrings. You can hang the little star from a simple silver chain or a solid silver-plated torque, or for a more formal look, hang it from a luxurious woven silver necklace, as shown here.

Twist and coil earrings

Twisting two lengths of wire together creates an interesting texture, and also makes the wire easier to coil. A spinster cord maker, available from craft stores, is normally used for making thread cord for needlecrafts, but it is also a useful little tool for twisting jewellery wire.

"Palatine is the name given to a particular shape of glass bead. These top-quality beads have a wonderful intensity and are available in a range of colours."

You will need

Materials

- 1.2 m (49 in) of 0.45 mm (26 swg) aqua enamelled wire
- 40 cm (16 in) of 0.2 mm (36 swg) silver-plated wire
- 16 size 9/00 aqua seed beads
- Two aqua palatine beads
- Two sterling silver earring hooks

Tools

- Flat-nose pliers or vice
- Round-nose pliers
- Spinster cord maker
- Safety goggles
- Ruler
- Wire cutters

1 Cut a 1.2 m (49 in) length of 0.45 mm (26 swg) wire and fold it in half. Put on safety goggles and clamp the cut ends of the wire in a vice, or ask a friend to hold the cut ends firmly in a pair of flat-nose pliers. Loop the other end of the wire over the hook of the spinster cord maker and twist until the wire is tightly twisted. Take care when releasing the wire from the pliers or vice in case the ends spring back.

Helpful hint
If you do not have a spinster cord maker, simply slip a pencil into the wire loop and turn the pencil around against your fist to twist the wire by hand.

★★☆ **Skill level**   🕐 **1-2 hours**   **Techniques:** *Bending wire p.16, Making a coil p.17, Attaching earring wires p.19*

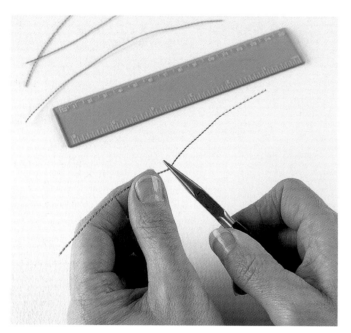

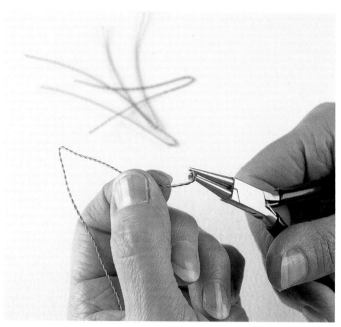

2 Cut two 12 cm (4³/₄ in) lengths and two 15 cm (6 in) lengths from the twisted wire. Hold each length against the ruler and grasp the centre point with the flat-nose pliers. Bend the wire over and then fold each length in half.

3 Hold one end of a 12 cm (4³/₄ in) folded wire in the round-nose pliers close to the tip so that the cut ends are level with the edge of the pliers. Bend the twisted wire around the pliers to form a loop. Hold onto the loop with the pliers and start to bend the wire around the loop to begin shaping the coil.

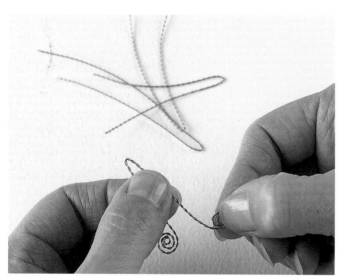

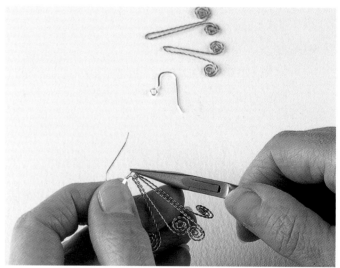

4 Hold the loop between your finger and thumb and continue to bend the wire around to form a small coil, about 7 mm (⁵/₁₆ in) in diameter. Make a loop on the other end of the wire so that it is facing in the opposite direction, then bend it around to make a coil the same size. Make similar sized coils on the other 12 cm (4³/₄ in) length and on each end of the longer lengths of twisted wire.

5 Using flat-nose pliers, twist open the ring at the end of the sterling silver earring hook and insert one long and one short piece of twisted wire. Close the hook again. Make a second earring to match.

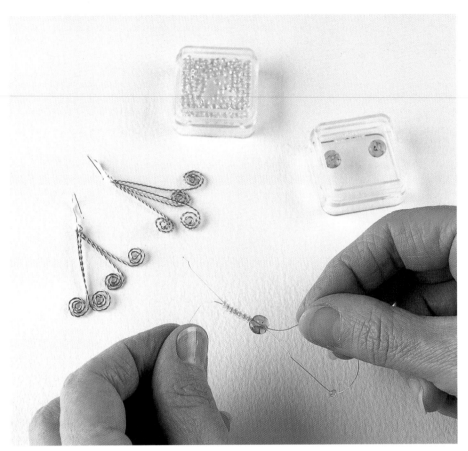

6 Cut a 20 cm (8 in) length of 0.2 mm (36 swg) silver-plated wire. Pick up seven seed beads, a palatine bead and another seed bead. Miss the last seed bead added and feed the wire up through the palatine bead and the seed beads. Wind the end around above the bead and trim off the excess. Feed the other end of the wire through the loop of the earring hook in front of the two twisted wire pieces. Feed the wire down through the seed beads, wrap around above the palatine and snip off the excess. Finish the second earring to match.

Variation

Twist and coil feather earrings

This pair of earrings is made in the same way as the main project. Form the alternative heart shape by making the coils as before, then crossing the wires over each other so that the coils lie side by side. There will be a small hoop at the top of each shape that can be fitted onto the earring hook. To attach the feather, wrap 0.2 mm (36 swg) silver-plated wire around the feather at the required length and trim the feather to length. Loop the wire through the earring hook and wrap it around the feather a few times to secure. Trim the excess wire. Make a second earring to match.

Small spiral bead bracelet

Spiral beads are usually made using a special coiling tool, but it is actually quite easy to make these beads using a rod or knitting needle. The thickness of the wire and the diameter of the rod or knitting needle will determine the size of the spiral bead.

"Brightly coloured enamelled wire makes these little spiral beads appear jewel-like. Choose crystals that complement the wire colour for best effect."

You will need

Materials

- 5 m (5 yds) of 0.2 mm (36 swg) turquoise enamelled wire
- Size 1.5 mm (size 000) knitting needle or 1.5 mm (1/16 in) rod
- 5m (5 yds) of 0.315 mm (30 swg) turquoise enamelled wire
- About ten 4 mm (1/6 in) blue crystals
- 20 cm (8 in) of bracelet memory wire
- Gel superglue

Tools

- Heavyweight wire cutters
- Flat-nose pliers

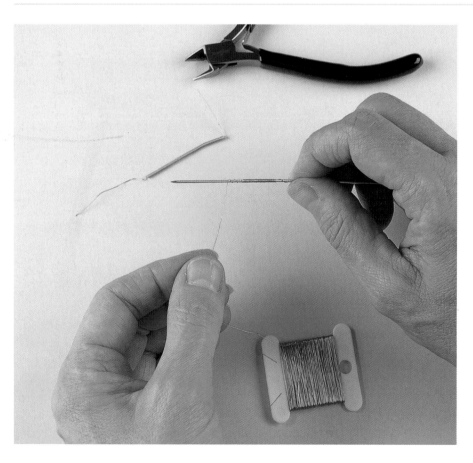

1 Hold the 0.2 mm (36 swg) turquoise wire against the knitting needle or rod and wrap it around about 110 times to make a tightly packed spring about 4 cm (1½ in) long. Cut the end and slide the spring off. Repeat to make ten springs the same length, and then trim all ends flush with the spring.

★★☆ **Skill level**   🕐 **1-2 hours**   **Techniques:** *Cutting wire p.15, Making a spiral p.18*

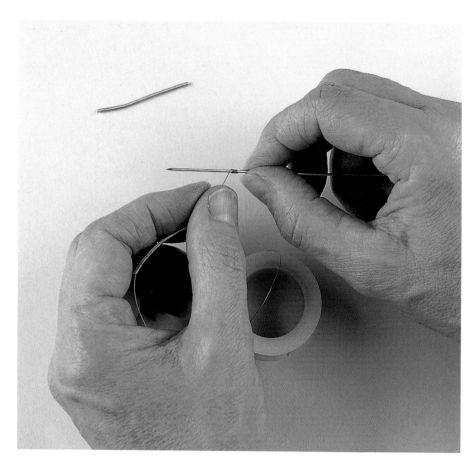

2 Feed one of the springs onto the 0.315 mm (30 swg) wire as it comes off the reel, and let it drop down slightly. Hold the wire against the knitting needle and wind it around six or seven times to form a tight coil.

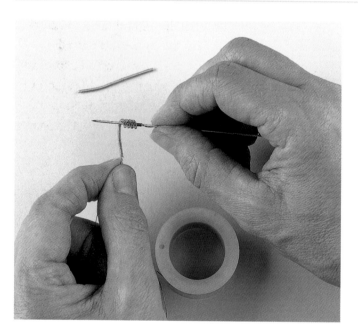

3 Let the wire spring drop down the wire to the knitting needle. Holding the tail against the needle, begin to wind the spring around to form a tight spiral. Once you get to the end of the spring, keep winding the thicker wire around six or seven times to form a tight spiral at this end as well.

4 Slide the spiral bead off the needle. Make another nine beads in the same way. Trim all of the wire ends off the beads.

5 Cut a round of memory wire slightly longer than you require. Pick up a crystal and apply a few drops of superglue onto the end of the wire. Slide the crystal along to the end of the wire and allow to dry.

Helpful hint
Memory wire is an extremely tough wire. Use heavyweight cutters to cut into it, as fine jewellery wire cutters will become damaged.

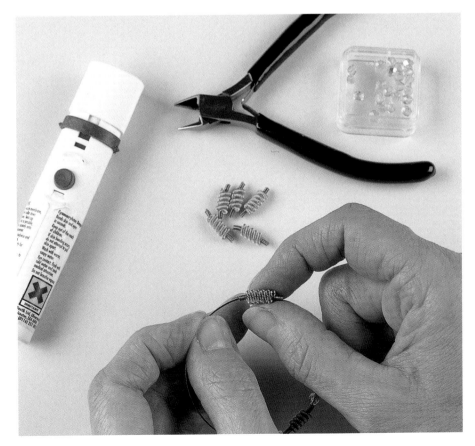

6 Slide a spiral bead on to the wire and then a crystal. Repeat until all the spiral beads are on the wire. Stick the last bead in position with super glue. Snip off the end of the memory wire flush with the last crystal.

Wire bead necklace

It looks almost impossible to get the beads inside the little wire baskets in this pretty necklace, but like all good tricks, there is a simple explanation. The baskets are made from coiled wire that is shaped to fit the bead and then bent into place with the bead inside.

"Frosted beads are available in a wide range of colours. The gorgeous matte surface of these beads contrasts beautifully with the shiny silver wire."

You will need

Materials

- 80 cm (31½ in) of 1 mm (19 swg) silver-plated wire
- Five 1 cm (⅝ in) purple frosted beads
- Silver-plated torque necklace
- Clear-setting epoxy resin
- Needle or cocktail stick

Tools

- Wire cutters
- Round-nose pliers
- Flat-nose pliers
- Ruler
- Permanent marker

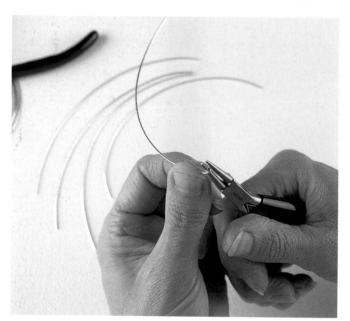

1 Cut five 16 cm (6¼ in) lengths of silver-plated wire. Hold one length in the round-nose pliers so that the end is flush with the jaws. Bend the end of the wire around the pliers using your thumb to guide it around until it touches the pliers again.

2 Holding the ring with the round-nose pliers, begin to bend the wire around to form the coil. Switch to flat-nose pliers and hold the coil flat between the jaws. Bend the tail around gently and then move the coil around in the pliers and bend again.

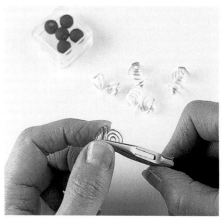

3 Continue bending and moving the coil until the tail measures 8 cm (3⅛ in). Make a ring in the other end of the wire and coil the end until the two coils meet in a "c" shape.

4 Hold each coil between your finger and thumb and twist in opposite directions to create an "s" shape. Use pliers to bend the coils in slightly so that they are level.

5 Bend the two coils toward one another until they are sitting at right angles. Hold the points of the flat-nose pliers in the centre of one coil. Hold your finger and thumb behind the coil and push the coil to create a small dome shape. Guide the shape with your finger and thumb. Repeat with the other coil.

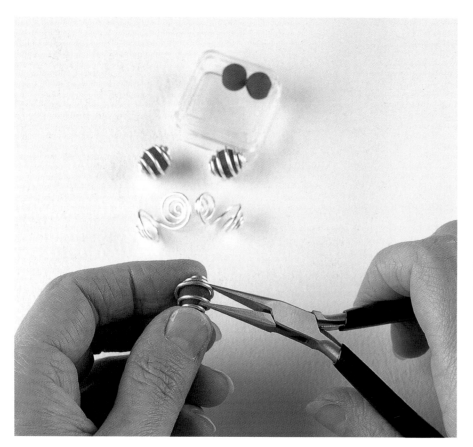

6 Insert the bead and push the two halves together. You will need to space the wires evenly with a pair of flat-nose pliers. Make another four coiled pieces of wire and fit a bead inside each one.

Helpful hint
Use a needle or a cocktail stick to manoeuvre the beads around inside the wire baskets so that the holes line up, ready to feed onto the torque necklace.

7 Mark the torque necklace with a permanent marker to show where the beads are going to sit. Slide the wired beads onto the torque necklace. Apply a small amount of epoxy resin on one of the outside marks and slide the bead into position. Hold the bead until the glue sets, then stick the remaining beads on, one at a time.

Variation

Wire bead earrings

To make these pretty earrings, make two wired beads as shown in steps 1-6 of the main project. Cut a 15 cm (6 in) length of silver-plated wire and make a loop at one end using round-nose pliers. Bend the tail back on itself slightly, until it is straight. Feed on a wired bead. Make a loop at the other side of the bead and snip off the tail. Fit an earring hook into one of the loops. Make a second earring to match.

Triangle silver necklace

These striking wire motifs are simply bent using your eye as a guide, although you can use the first motif as a template for all the rest. Practise bending a few motifs so that you know exactly where to hold the pliers to create the desired shape.

"Use oval rather than round jump rings to link the bent wire motifs together, as oval rings are flatter and look more attractive with this style of necklace."

You will need

Materials

- 2.5 m (2³/₄ yds) of 1 mm (19 swg) silver-plated wire
- Tissue
- Ten 6 x 4 mm (¹/₄ x ¹/₈ in) silver-plated oval jump rings
- Silver necklace fitment

Tools

- Wire cutters
- Flat-nose pliers (two pairs optional)
- Round-nose pliers
- Ruler

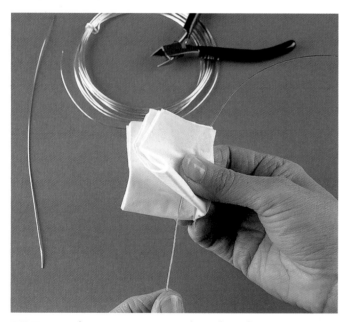

1 Cut eleven 20 cm (8 in) lengths of 1 mm (19 swg) silver-plated wire. If the wire has been cut from a coil or reel, it must be straightened before being bent into shape. To do this, pull the lengths of wire through a tissue, exerting gentle pressure with your thumb to take the curve out of the wire.

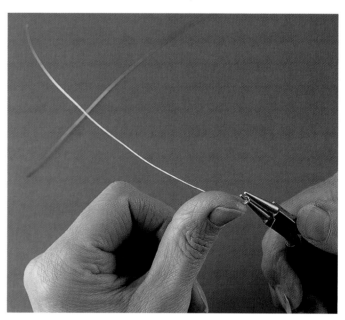

2 Trim the wire at one end. Using round-nose pliers, hold the wire so that it is flush with the edge of the pliers. Bend the wire around the pliers by applying some pressure with your thumb to form a tight loop.

★★★ **Skill level**   🕐 **2-3 hours**   **Techniques:** *Straightening wire p.15, Bending wire p.16, Turning a loop p.16*

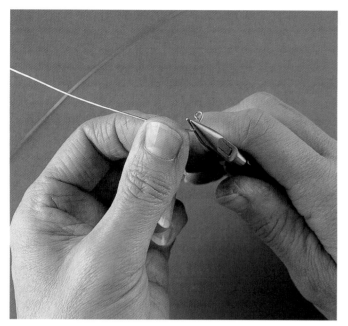

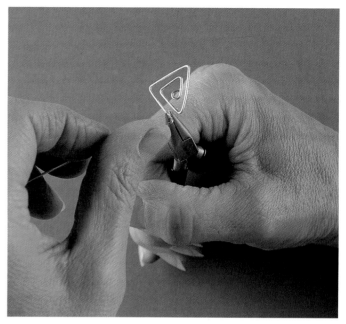

3 Hold the wire close to the loop with flat-nose pliers and bend it against the pliers to create a corner 5 mm (¼ in) from the loop. Bend the wire again about 9 mm (³⁄₈ in) from the previous corner.

4 Continue bending the wire so that a triangle is formed with the wires about 3-4mm (¹⁄₈-¹⁄₆ in) apart. Bend five corners in all to create one half of the diamond motif. Bend the wire in the opposite direction along the base of the triangle to begin the other side.

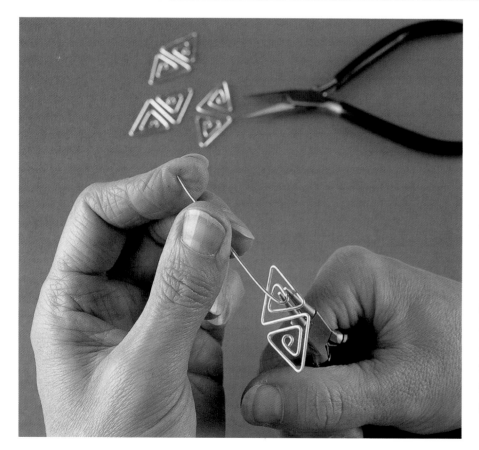

5 Judge by eye to create the second bend. Continue bending the wire to make progressively smaller triangles. After the fifth bend, switch to the round-nose pliers and bend the wire around the tip of the pliers to form a loop. Snip off the end and flatten into position with flat-nose pliers. Make a further ten diamond motifs.

Helpful hint
When bending to fit progressively smaller triangles inside the previous ones, hold the pliers 1 mm (¹⁄₁₆ in) back from where you intend the wire to bend to allow for the thickness of the wire.

6 Open out one of the oval jump rings and insert two of the diamond motifs (see page 18). Make sure both pieces are facing in the same direction. Close the loops. Join all the wire motifs together in the same way. Fit a necklace fitment on each end.

Variation

Triangle silver earrings

These triangle wire motifs can be used to make an elegant set of earrings to match the necklace. Simply form two wire motifs and attach an earring hook to one end, then do the same to make the other earring. While silver wire gives a classic look, you can also use gold-plated wire or a coloured enamelled wire for a completely different effect.

Wire jig earrings

The subtle silver-plated wire used for these earrings beautifully showcases the wonderful sparkle of the Swarovski crystals. Not to be confused with less expensive pressed glass beads, these stunning crystals are available in a range of different colours, shapes, sizes and finishes.

"Wire jigs come in a variety of shapes, and each has a different layout of holes, allowing you to create a multitude of wire shapes for jewellery."

You will need

Materials

- 40 cm (16 in) of 0.8 mm (21 swg) silver-plated wire
- 1 m (1 yd) of 0.375 mm (28 swg) silver-plated wire
- Six each of 4 mm (⅛ in) Swarovski crystals in AB (Aurora Borealis) moonlight, lilac and purple
- Pair of sterling silver earring hooks

Tools

- Wire jig with medium pegs
- Wire cutters
- Flat-nose pliers
- Round-nose pliers
- Ruler

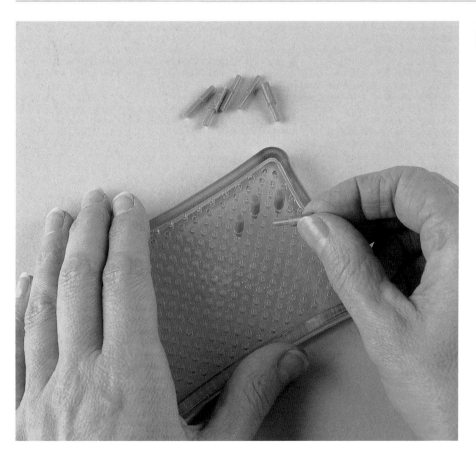

1 Insert two medium pegs into the wire jig so that there are two empty holes between them. Insert two medium pegs vertically in the middle of the first two pegs to form an elongated diamond.

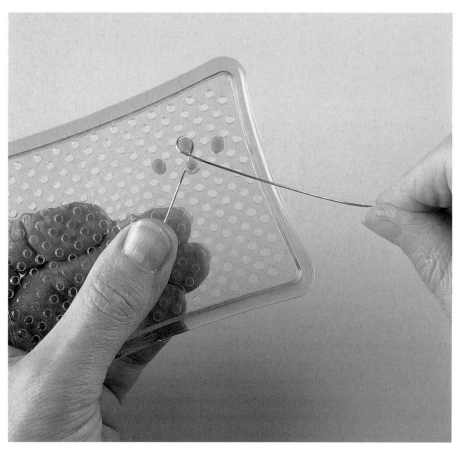

2 Cut a 20 cm (8 in) length of 0.8 mm (21 swg) wire. Hold one end of the wire flat against the wire jig with your left thumb so that the wire lies diagonally across the pegs. Hold the other end of the wire and bend it around the top peg. Gently pull on the end of wire so that it comes off the peg in the opposite direction in a straight line diagonally across the pegs.

Helpful hint
The 0.8 mm (21 swg) wire is ideal for this project because it holds its shape. To make it easier to exert more pressure in order to bend the wire, hold on to the top of the peg as you bend the wire around it.

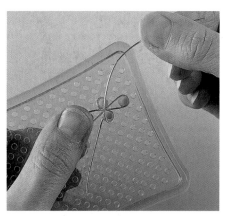

3 Loop the wire around the bottom of the right-hand peg, round the top of the right-hand peg and then diagonally around the left-hand peg. Continue to maintain the tension without pulling the pegs out. Finish by bending the wire around the bottom peg and back across the pegs diagonally to complete the wire jig motif.

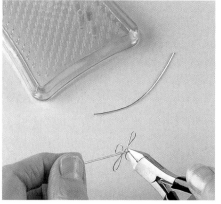

4 Lift the wire motif off the wire jig. Flatten the wire shape gently with flat-nose pliers. Snip the tails off the top and bottom hoops where the wires cross over. Ease one of the loops over to the other side of the motif so that the diagonal wire goes across the front of the wire jig motif. Make a second motif in the same way.

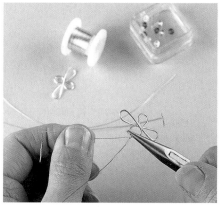

5 Cut three 15 cm (6 in) lengths of 0.375 mm (28 swg) silver-plated wire. Feed one length through the bottom centre loop twice and pull tight. Hold the wire jig motif in the flat-nose pliers so that the looped wire is secure.

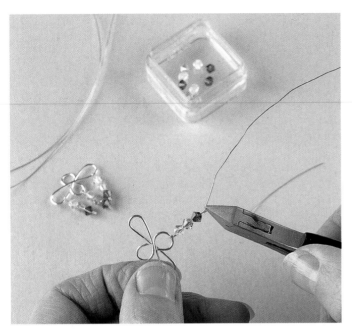

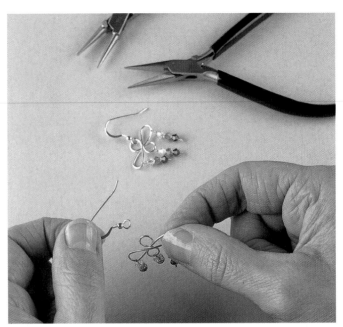

6 Wrap one end of the wire around the other four or five times to form a tight wrapping. Hold both wires together and feed on three crystals, one in each colour, beginning with the lightest shade. Repeat the wrapping below the crystals and then snip both wires off neatly.

7 Wrap another length of the 0.375 mm (28 swg) wire around each of the long loops and add three crystals to each length in exactly the same way as before. Finish the second earring to match. Using flat-nose pliers, twist open the loops on a pair of sterling silver earring hooks and fit the completed motifs.

Variations

Wire jig design ideas

There are innumerable different designs that you can create with a wire jig. Simply arrange the pegs and twist the wire around them. When you are trying out wire jig designs for the first time, it is quicker to test out different shapes if you use a 0.5-0.6 mm (25-23 swg) wire, as this wire gauge is easier to bend. Remember to change to a thicker wire to make the actual earrings.

Dragonfly brooch

With their shimmering iridescent bodies, dragonflies look stunning as they flit about around the countryside fluttering their beautiful silvery wings. This gorgeous brooch is so realistic that when pinned on a lapel or your favourite hat, it will look like a real dragonfly has stopped for a rest.

"In this artistic brooch, three different coloured tubes of knitting are fitted one inside the other to recreate the iridescent colours of a dragonfly's body."

You will need

Materials

- 50 cm (20 in) of 0.5 mm (25 swg) silver-plated wire
- 5 m (5 yds) of 0.315 mm (30 swg) silver-plated wire
- 0.315 mm (30 swg) Wyr Knittr jewel pack (contains cyclamen pink, peacock blue and aqua wire)
- 0.6 mm (24 swg) aqua wire
- Two 5 mm (¼ in) blue frosted beads
- Clear-setting epoxy resin

- Brooch fastening or silver-plated hat pin

Tools

- Flat-nose pliers
- Wire cutters
- Ruler
- Wyr Knittr or French knitting tool
- Embroidery scissors
- Bodkin or needle

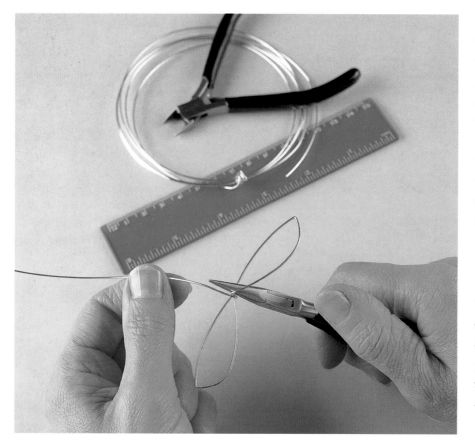

1 Cut a 50 cm (20 in) length of 0.5 mm (25 swg) silver-plated wire. Bend the wire at 90 degrees 5 cm (2 in) from one end, and again about 8 cm (3 in) away. Bend the wire end back towards the middle and wind it around two or three times to secure. Shape the top edges of the wings into a soft curve between your finger and thumb.

Helpful hint
For the dragonfly to look fairly realistic, the proportions should be somewhat correct. Use the photograph opposite as a guide to make the wings and body the right shapes and relative lengths.

2 Create the last wing by bending the wire up at 90 degrees and curving the wire back around to the middle. Hold the wings in the middle with a pair of flat-nose pliers. Wind the tail end around the middle of the lower wings two or three times to secure, then snip off the end.

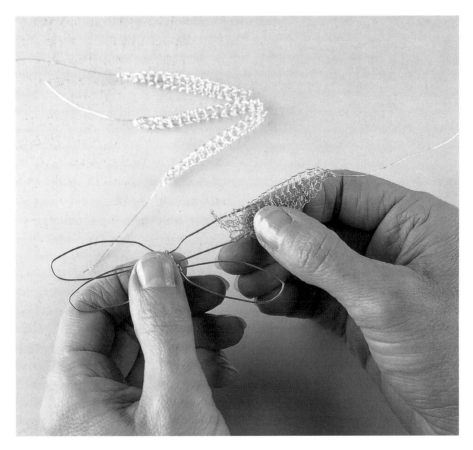

3 Using a Wyr Knittr or French knitting tool, knit a 20 cm (8 in) length of tubing using the 0.315 mm (30 swg) silver-plated wire. Cut the tube into four equal pieces. Unravel some of the wire from the cut pieces and feed it through the loops to finish the ends. Open the tubes out slightly by inserting embroidery scissors inside and gently opening the blades. Slide the flattened tubes one at a time over the wings and push the ends into shape. Weave in the tail and snip off the end.

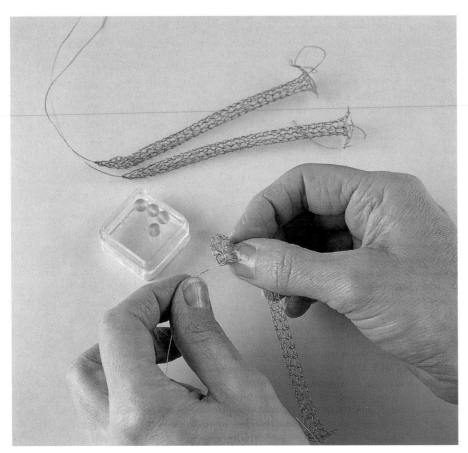

4 To make the dragonfly's body, knit a 10 cm (4 in) length of tubing with each of the pink, aqua and blue wires. Push the two blue beads into the hole at the top of the aqua knitted tube and then wind the end of the wire around below the beads so that they end up sitting side by side.

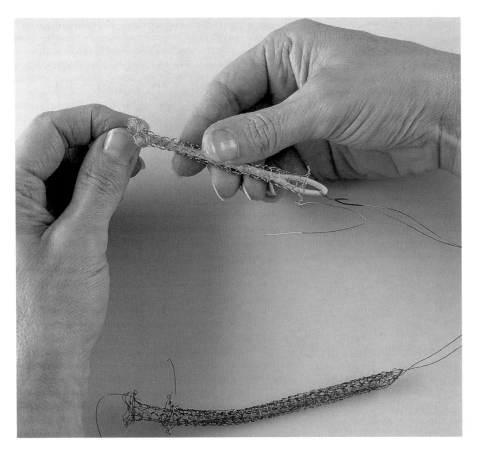

5 Roll the pink knitted tube between your hands to make it a little thinner, then thread the wire end onto a bodkin or needle. Feed the bodkin or needle up through the blue tube and pull the pink wire inside. Roll both of these tubes to narrow them slightly, then thread on the bodkin or needle and feed both tubes into the aqua knitted tube, bringing the wires out between the blue beads.

6 Wrap the pink and blue wires between the beads and around the neck several times to create the dragonfly's head. Continue wrapping the wire around below the beads to make a short, fat neck area. You may need to attach a bit more wire in order to achieve the right effect.

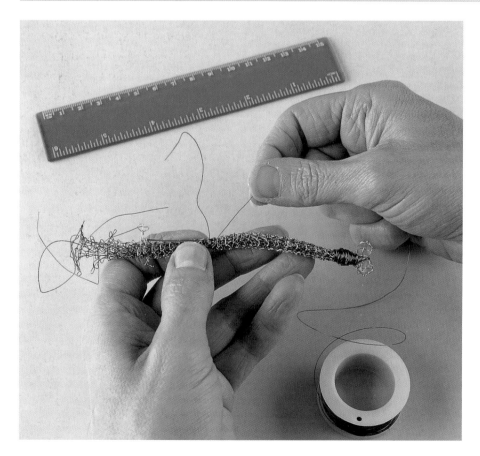

7 Insert a length of 0.6 mm (24 swg) aqua wire down the centre of the dragonfly's body. Wrap 0.315 mm (30 swg) pink wire around the long body about six or seven times, about 7 cm (2³/₄ in) below the eyes. Secure the end, then trim off the excess wire and tubing below the wrapping.

8 Cut three 5 cm (2 in) lengths of 0.6 mm (24 swg) aqua wire for the legs. Using flat-nose pliers, bend each of the three pieces of aqua wire in the middle to form two legs.

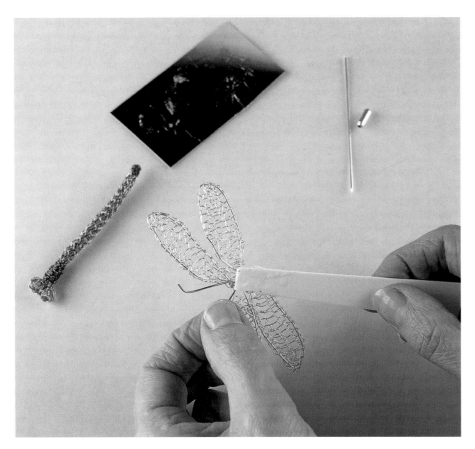

9 Secure the legs to the back of the wings, one under the other, with a few dots of epoxy resin. Glue the dragonfly's body on top of the wings and leave to dry. To make a hatpin or a lapel pin, feed a silver-plated hatpin in at the back of the dragonfly's body, just below the eyes, and bring it out somewhere in the upper section of the body. Apply a few drops of glue over the top of the pin to hold it in place. To use as a brooch, glue a brooch fastening onto the back of the dragonfly's wings.

Cone necklace

No special tools are necessary to make the cone-shaped wire decoration on this necklace. It is made simply by wrapping wire around the blades of a pair of round-nose pliers. The lustre of the gold-plated wire looks wonderful next to the gorgeous orange crystals.

"If you don't want to make cone-shaped decorations, you could make a very simple, yet charming necklace using only beads and wire links."

You will need

Materials
- 5 m (5 yds) of 0.7 mm (22 swg) gold-plated wire
- About 50 4 mm (⅙ in) orange crystals
- Gold-plated lobster claw clasp

Tools
- Round-nose pliers
- Flat-nose pliers
- Wire cutters
- Ruler

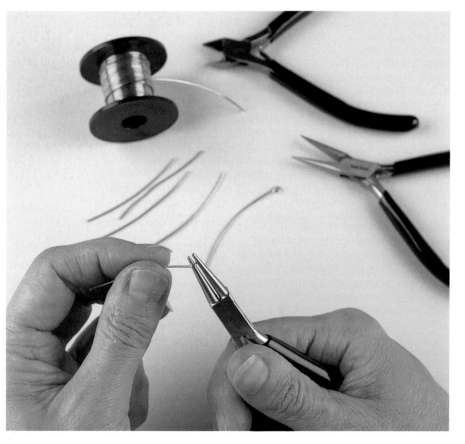

1 Cut 42 5 cm (2 in) lengths of gold-plated wire. Using a pair of round-nose pliers, grasp a length of wire so that the end is flush with the edge of the pliers and bend the wire around using the thumb of your other hand. Change to flat-nose pliers and insert the points into the ring. Bend the tail end back slightly until the ring is straight. Repeat with the other pieces of wire.

Helpful hint
It is quicker to cut all 42 pieces of wire and form all of the links at the same time, rather than making one complete bead link at a time.

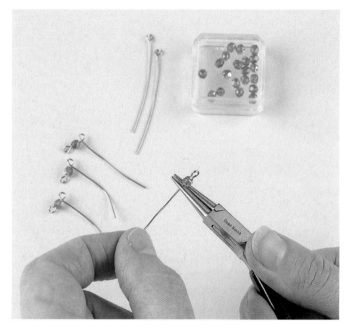

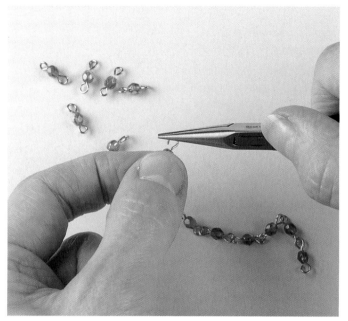

2   Feed a crystal onto the wire. Using a pair of round-nose pliers, hold the wire just above the crystal. Bend the wire around the point of the pliers to create a ring. Repeat with the other wires.

3   Trim the excess wire from each beaded link and, using flat-nose pliers, line both rings up so that they are facing in the same direction. Open one end of the first beaded link and join to the next, then close to secure. Continue adding links until the necklace is the length required.

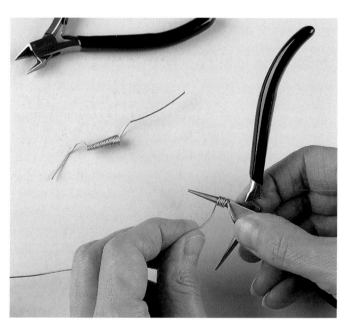

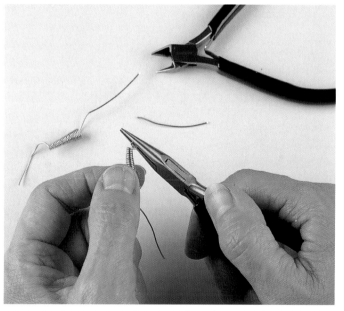

4   To make the cone-shaped decoration, hold the end of the gold-plated wire as it comes off the reel against the side of the round-nose pliers. Wind the wire around the blade of the pliers to make a tightly packed cone of wire. Make five cones in all.

5   Make a ring at the top of each cone shape using round-nose pliers. Snip off the excess wire and bend the ring into position so that it is level with the back edge of the cone.

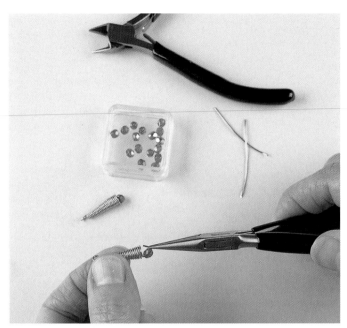

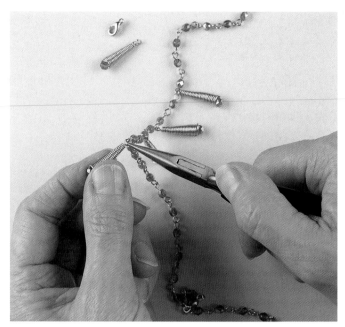

6 Bend the wire at the bottom of the cone so that it is facing across the base of the cone. Feed a crystal onto the wire and snip off the excess wire so that it measures 6 mm (¹⁄₄ in). Bend this tail against the side of the bead and push into the cone.

7 Fit a decorative cone into one of the link rings in the centre of the chain. Fit two more cones on either side of the centre, leaving a gap of two links, followed by two more cones after another two-link gap. Fit a lobster claw clasp onto one side. Use the last bead link ring to receive the fastening.

Variation

Dangly cone earrings

The two elements that make up this necklace can easily be used to make a matching pair of earrings. Simply make a bead link and a cone-shaped decoration for each earring. Attach the link to the top of the cone shape, and then fit an earring wire to the other end of the bead link. You can, of course, make the earrings in any colour you wish. Look out for coloured enamelled wire, as shown here, for a more colourful take on this design.

Suppliers

UNITED KINGDOM

The Bead Shop
104-106 Upper Parliament Street
Nottingham
NG1 6LF
Tel: 0115 9588899
Email: info@mailorder-beads.co.uk
www.mailorder-beads.co.uk
Beads, equipment and findings

Constellation Beads
The Coach House
Barningham
Richmond
North Yorkshire
DL11 7DW
Tel: 01833 621094
Email:
        info@constellationbeads.co.uk
www.constellationbeads.co.uk
Mail-order bead company

Creative Beadcraft
20 Beak Street
London
W1R 3HA
Tel: 020 7629 9964
Mail order tel: 01494 778818
Email: beads@creativebeadcraft.co.uk
www.creativebeadcraft.co.uk
Beads, equipment and findings

Homecrafts Direct
PO Box 38
Leicestershire LE1 9BU
Tel: 0845 458 4531
www.homecraftsdirect.co.uk
General wire supplies

H. S. Walsh & Sons Ltd
44 Hatton Garden
London
EC1N 8ER
Tel: 020 7242 3711
Ring bending pliers, parallel pliers

Oliver Twists
22 Phoenix Road
Crowther
Washington
Tyne and Wear
NE38 0AD
Tel: 0191 4166016
Fax: 0191 4153405
Wire and embroidery thread

Ribbon Designs
PO Box 382
Edgware
Middlesex
HA8 7XQ
Tel/fax: 0208 958 4966
Email: info@silkribbon.co.uk
*Metallic and organdie embroidery
ribbons*

The Scientific Wire Company
18 Raven Road
London
E18 1HW
Tel: 0208 505 0002
Fax: 0208 559 1114
www.wires.co.uk
Wire and bullion

The Spellbound Bead Company
45 Tamworth Street
Lichfield
Staffordshire
WS13 6JW
Tel: 01543 417650
www.spellboundbead.co.uk

21st Century Beads
Craft Workshops
South Pier Road
Ellesmere Port
Cheshire
CH65 4FW
Tel: 0151 356 4444
Fax: 0151 355 3377
www.beadmaster.com
Beads, equipment and findings

AUSTRALIA

Bead Werks
100 Ryrie St.
Geelong,
Victoria 3220
Tel: 03 5221 0988
Fax: 03 5221 0988
E-mail: ddhiggins@bigpond.com

Beads n Crystals
Mayfair Arcade
126 Adelaide Street
Brisbane,
Queensland 4000
Tel: 07 3220 0882
Fax: (07) 3220 1441
Beads, crystals and wire jigs

The Bead Gallery
Shop 3, Lakes Central
Corner of Woolcock Street and
    Kings Road
Westend,
Townsville
QLD 4810
Tel: 07 4721 1122

The Bead World Warehouse
Bead World International
1/7 Villiers Drive
Currumbin
QLD 4223
Tel: 07 5534 1333
www.beadworld-international.com

Lincraft
Head Office
31–33 Alfred Street
Blackbun
VIC 3130
Tel: 03 9875 7575
*General craft supplies, outlets
nationwide*

Over the Rainbow Jewellery Supplies
P.O. Box 495
Ascot Vale
 Victoria 3032
Tel: 03 9376 0545

NEW ZEALAND

Auckland Beads
POC: Linley Main
PO Box 32-616,
Devonport,
Auckland
Tel: 09 445 3500
Fax 09 446 6443
Email: linley.main@xtra.co.nz

Bead Me Up
1184 Hinemoa Street
Rotorua
Tel: 07 349 0844
Fax: 07 349 1082
Email: rozcraft@iconz.co.nz
www.craftwarehouse.co.nz

Beads and Pieces
297 Ponsonby Road
Ponsonby, Auckland
Tel: 09 376 1030
and
56 Broadway
Newmarket, Auckland
Tel: 09 529 5455
Beads and findings specialist

Bead Gallery
18 Parere Street
Nelson
Tel: 03 546 7807
www.beads.co.nz
Beads and findings specialist

SOUTH AFRICA

Art, Stock & Barrel
Shop 44, Parklane Centre
12 Commercial Road
Pietermaritzburg 3201
Tel: 033 342 1026

Bead Sales
223 Long Street
Cape Town
Tel: 021 423 4687
Mail order fax: 021 422 1773
General bead supplies

The Bead Shop
89 First Avenue
Melville, Johannesburg
Tel: 011 726 2911
Mail order service

Crafty Arts
Walmer Park Shopping Centre
Port Elizabeth 6001
Tel: 041 368-2528

Crafty Supplies
Shop UG 2, Stadium on Main
Claremont 7700
Cape Town
Tel: 021 671-0286

Index